OM DIVINE GRACE YOGA

The Goddess Power

Paramhansa Ganesh Giri

Copyright © 2024 Author *Paramhansa Ganesh Giri*
Cover Art – *Yogi Dream*. (Authors acrylic art)

All rights reserved.
ISBN: 978-0-473-71690-5

Contents

Introduction	Pg. i
Chapter 1 – The Yogic Pathway	Pg. 1
Chapter 2 – *Kundalini & Shakti*	Pg. 23
Chapter 3 – The *Siddha &* Divine Grace	Pg. 46
Chapter 4 – My Indian journey	Pg. 75
Chapter 5 – After India	Pg. 93
Chapter 6 – Post - Enlightenment	Pg. 117
Chapter 7 – The Challenge	Pg. 145
Chapter 8 – Being Divine	Pg. 173
Appendix	Pg. 190

Born Raymond Pattison - aged 18 became a "holy man".

(A Sadhu, in India).

I became – Paramahamsa Ganesh Giri

I lived in India for 10 years

Divine Grace Yoga – Mantra Shakti

Introduction
Om Divine Grace Yoga
(Mantra Shakti Yoga)

This Yogic Pathway:
Om Divine Grace Yoga is about the Goddess Power – *Shakti* in Sanskrit. Its foundation is the power of *Mantras.*
This a "Pathway Manual".
Comprises four sections. The content has been written in a general way in different parts of my previous books. However, now, this pathway is distilled into more specific practices and presented as this workbook/manual/guidebook. This is a spiritual practitioner reference source and guide for those interested in exploring this pathway.
The contents will further enable the spiritual practitioner to complete a pathway leading to *Enlightenment or Self-Realization.* There is no intent to promote this pathway above, beyond, or superior to any other spiritual practice. It is simply a means that could be divinely useful if followed. It is also a system based on traditional and ancient spiritual and religious practices from the East. Interestingly, some components, such as *Mantra* use, *Kundalini,* and *Chakras* have become embedded in Westernized, spiritual practice to a

point where they are not necessarily identified as belonging to a religion such as Hinduism.

It's all about the Power or *Shakti* of the Goddess, (or *Devi*), that presents to me in the form of given Mantras, which I have used for fifty plus years

It's also:

Devi Shakti Marg - देवी शक्ति मार्ग

Devī (Sanskrit: देवी), is the Sanskrit word for *Goddess*.
Shakti approximately means "power/energy".
Shakti is understood to be the active dimension of the Goddess
Mārga, (मार्ग), *refers to the* course *or* "pathway".

Divine Grace Yoga - Mantra Shakti

Chapter 1

Om Guru Om

The word *Guru* is easy to explain.
Gu means darkness and *Ru* means light.
Tune into the teachers around you, and you are moving from darkness into light
Maybe in the beginning it's just a bit of learning about how to do something different spiritually, but it's still a significant step into the spiritual process.

Engage with the *Sat Guru* or True Teacher process in depth, then we're talking about another planet. Not the current human experience within *Life and the Universe,* (which is in a dark age known as *Kali Yuga*). This is about going beyond the light and the dark. You are entitled to participate in this process, as a Divine Being in essence.

Divine Grace Yoga - Mantra Shakti

Forget about what religions and so-called enlightened teachers try to enforce. (Telling you that they are fully enlightened or divine, and you are just an ordinary human).

There's a reason why religions and cults are essentially giving teachings that are often impossible to follow. You go to hell if you don't comply, so now they have your attention! Go to any of the teachers, religions, whatever, and they will say even if you get enlightened, you stay as you are and need to remain being a devoted follower. A servant or a follower of that particular religion/guru, who says you can't get to his level. (Usually it's a "he"). It's about control.

It might be hard to have radical views about one's own spirituality. This is not about being a monk or a monastic person or anyway retiring or being separate from whatever you're doing now. This is about you being essentially already a Divine Being in your current situation, no matter what. (Crazy, addict, atheist, lost, and depressed, or maybe "doing ok"). You don't have to be stable to start this journey!

Thus, the pathway and perspectives outlined herein will move on from the labels, and look at your Divinity, and your strengths, and your ability to function at a recognizable *spiritual level* within the current planet that you're on. Here is the essence of this *Yogic Pathway.*

Mantra Shakti Yoga consists of four components:

- ***MANTRA YOGA***
  Using mantras for Enlightenment.
  The mantra seeks to make our enlightenment a practical experience.
  Something we can do through the body and mind down to the tips of our toes and through all emotional mental and physical states.
  The type of mantra that will work requires that we understand the *chakra* centers of our body.
- ***KUNDALINI YOGA***
  Kundalini as the "serpent" energy flows up and down between the body centers.
  In Sanskrit these are called chakras, which translates as "wheel".
  It's a center that takes in and gives out energy
  Traditionally there are mantra like sounds associated with the chakras, plus there are "secret" *Bija,* (seed) mantras.

Divine Grace Yoga - Mantra Shakti

The Bija mantras allow access to the energy of the chakras to move negative energy up and out of the body. Also, then Divine energies move down to the specific chakra that is being focused upon.

This focus is achieved with specific seed mantras for each chakra.

- ***SHAKTI YOGA***

    The seed mantras are allied to the Goddess Energy and to the spiritual path of Shakti, (Divine Energy seen as female in presentation).

    They are in essence *Tantric* mantras. The word *Tantra* means: "go out into the world", or "to weave"'. *Tantra Yoga* simply is about applying the spiritual processes, so as to be out in the world instead of seeking introspection.

    By using seed mantras which relate both to specific Shakti forms, and to a chakra, we can infuse our yoga practice throughout the whole body.

    As we meditate on all the chakras and their Shakti connection, we release the negative power and receive the Divine Power.

    (Tantric mantras can produce awakening of the Kundalini, the primal energy of Shakti).

- ***SIDDHA YOGA***

    The spiritual journey is open to anyone at any time. There are no rules which say you must have a guide, a teacher or a guru. The word guru means "one who leads from darkness to light". A guru must be already in the light to be able to reach out and help others to attain the same illumination. A guru can only affect others to the degree of that guru's own achievement. An enlightened guru can be a *Siddha Guru*. Siddha means: "with full yogic powers".

The spiritual aspirant will submit the dross, the mundane, and the un-enlightened mentality for the guru's inspection. The guru prescribes the "medicine" and the aspirant then moves on to the next stage - whether to take the "medicine" or not.

When the guru is approached in the appropriate manner, then the guru becomes the means for rapid progress on the spiritual journey. A *Sat Guru* is One Enlightened in Truth Awareness and is therefore a Siddha. This knowledgeable awareness can be "transmitted" by the Sat Guru to a student, by subtle means that are not easily understood by a novice. In Sanskrit the word for this transmission is *Shakti-Paat*, which is the transmission of Shakti energy by the Sat Guru to awaken the Kundalini. In Hinduism and Buddhism this energy transference is known to also awaken the "third eye" and allows the sleeping Kundalini force to rise up through the spine with a serpent like movement.

Divine Grace Yoga - Mantra Shakti

You can choose your cat to be your guru, indeed as you can choose any person as a teacher. However, if you wanted to learn to fly a jumbo jet would you take lessons from a bus driver? The importance of finding a Sat Guru may be overlooked or ignored in haste to develop one's spiritual experience within a short-term timeframe. (Rather than looking at the need for a long-term, solid, and productive pathway).

Processes occurring as a result of practice of the four Yogas

The spiritual growth may at times seem to increase negative emotions.

When the chakras are awakened the negative energies within them "come out".

The tendency is that addictions, fear, depression, and anxiety etc. can bubble to the surface, and thus create apparent problems. (Eventually though these are eliminated through the Crown Chakra at the top of the head).

This is a clearing process, but it can seem difficult - temporarily.

It can be also problematic if a person practices Tantric Kundalini awakening, (& perhaps uses seed mantras), without guidance. Mental disturbance can ensue.

Divine Grace Yoga - Mantra Shakti

Mantras I use with the Chakras
(The fundamental cornerstone)

The topmost chakra, the Crown Chakra, (and also the *Ajna Chakra* between the eyes), is allied to the "benchmark" mantra AUM or OM, which is also a seed mantra. The prime mantra of them all!
OM is not specific to female/male energy.
This is the sound of the universe, the Cosmic Soul that transcends everything. Traditionally it was theoretically the "only" key mantra for renunciate monks, or *Sannyasins*, as it enhances focus on the formless, transcendent to the world and human life. Using it on its own one can achieve awareness or knowledge of the formless God/Higher Power/Cosmic Consciousness.
In descending order after the crown plus the "third eye" chakra, comes the energy of Sarasvati, (the Goddess of learning) and is based in the throat.
Then the Maya energy in the heart chakra. *Maya or Mahamaya* as the Goddess, is the loci of our illusion, the world and the created universe. Seems real! Then it

Divine Grace Yoga - Mantra Shakti

seems to change, then vanish. Our dreams disappear. Our lives disappear! It's real enough for the unenlightened person, but really, we are not solid bodies at all! (Check Quantum physics plus the scientific perspective regarding the atom "dance" of so-called solid matter).

Next chakra is associated with the Goddess of wealth, in the navel area, extending around the stomach area. *Lakshmi* is the Goddess energy associated here. This energy includes also wealth and "food".

Then the two lower chakras are associated with the sexual energies and also the "dark" Goddess Kali.

Mantras I use for each chakra
Sahasraram Chakra - Crown Chakra - OM
Ajna Chakra - 3rd eye - OM
Vishuddha Chakra -Throat Chakra -Aim - (Aiim)
Anahata Chakra - Heart Chakra – Hrim – (Hreem)
Manipura Chakra - Solar plexus Chakra – Srim _ (Shreem)
Svadhisthana Chakra - "Sex" Chakra – Krim –(Kriim)
Muladhara Chakra - "Sex" Chakra – Klim - (Kliim)

The repetition, (*Japa*), of the above seed mantras, is allied specific to each chakra. This method is not found easily in ancient traditions and is quite a secret teaching! (Pronunciation as above).

Om or AUM has always been associated with the third eye or the spot between the eyebrows even when it has not been associated with Kundalini energy or chakras. It is also connected to the Crown Chakra, especially when the sound "trails off" into a long "Mmm". AH is also for the Crown Chakra, but practitioners of OM chanting may wish to focus on the final drawn out "M" sound of OM, trailing out of the crown and then out to the ether. This is a very powerful meditation, which may not come easily until other centres have been purified using other sounds.

OM is thus the most well know and expansive of the seed mantras as it leads into the "soundless" space, to formless *Samadhi*. (Deepest meditation without thought forms). It can cause the Shakti energy to surge upward and outward beyond the Kundalini Chakras. It is a domain where there is a subtle vibration that signifies the Transcendental Divinity. Om proceeds from deep down in the body at the level of the stomach and moves up towards the chakra between the eyebrows, and terminates with what is called the *Chandrabindu*, ("the point on the moon"). This is shown above the *M* letter like a quarter moon with a dot above it. The *M* sound moves into a subtle vibration and ends with that dot which is one with the Divine.

Other seed mantras also end with the Chandrabindu. However, their meanings are somewhat complex, because it is necessary to understand their connection with the energy form of Shakti in a specific chakra. The seed mantras are part of Tantric lore, Goddess worship, Shakti/ Kundalini energy in a broad sense. Thus, the seed mantras should also be considered in terms of both external focused meditation and for the "reverse" flow of energy back down the body through the chakras. This is an essential concept of Tantra and helps spirituality to be also external life based.

More about the seed mantras

Om (Source of all). Then Aim, Hrim, Srim, Krim, Klim

AIM – (pronounce Aiim), the Bija mantra of *Saraswati*, the goddess of learning.

HRIM - (pronounced Hreem), is the mantra of the Divine Maya. Through it we can control the illusion power of our own minds. Mahamaya is the goddess of power over the created universe. (Maya means "illusion" - approximately).

SHRIM - (pronounced Shreem), is a mantra of love, devotion and beauty, relating to *Lakshmi*, the Goddess of Beauty and Divine Grace, who gives us the good things of life, including health. It aids in fertility and rejuvenation. Lakshmi is the goddess of wealth (in its broadest sense).

KRIM - (pronounced Kreem), is the great mantra of *Kali*, has a special power relative to the lower chakras, which can both stimulate and transform. It a main mantra of the Tantra. It should be used with care. Kali, the fierce goddess, has the power to destroy.

KLIM – (pronounce Kliim), the seed mantra of *Kameshwari*, the goddess of desire or contentment and satisfaction.

OM AIM HRIM SHRIM KRIM KLIM

(In that descending order – see summary also in Appendix)

These seed mantras could be used for personal wish or desire gratification. In Tantric views this is not necessarily "bad' – just practice at a base level. Ultimately in the Tantric view, such diversions are temporary, as the repetition of mantra will always want to lead to the high purified spiritual levels. At such levels one is moved more into the heart and higher chakras, and the Divine etheric space, above and around. Then the mantras of choice would change.

OM or SOHAM are preferred.

Soham: So, signifies God or Guru, and Hum signifies oneself. Repetition is an acknowledgement of one's essential oneness with God and one's spiritual teacher. It is to be repeated as one takes a breath in for the first part, and as one exhales for the second. It is also to be repeated when one is already in a quiet calm space, which may require use of other spiritual exercises. With this mantra one can enter into an extremely deep transcendental calmness. The process of repetition with awareness of breath and deep meditation practice is the path of perfection – the *Siddha Yoga*.

Mantras to: *Get Enlightened.*

The contentious issue regarding mantra is initiation. Historically, mantras, were initiated by a Guru. In our modern world this might not be feasible or practical, given the nature of this dark era (Kali Yuga). It is necessary now to offer mantras as an option for any practitioner, desiring to use a mantra for spiritual progress. Thus, a mantra such as Om Guru Om can be used immediately. Guru means "going from darkness to light", and this mantra repetition enables the reception of the inner guidance. Such guidance comes from the Inner Guru, which can be accessed to get "initiation" of other mantras. Om Guru Om is a benign mantra with no after-effects, other than receiving sobering thoughts and guidance. Becoming aware of one's previous negative activities is spiritually "good". Other mantras such as the seed mantras can be risky without clarity of use. Even so they can be used with right

Divine Grace Yoga - Mantra Shakti

understanding, as per the further information and instruction on this topic. Also, as a result of receiving Divine Guidance from within there will be appropriate additional clarity. It just requires good intent and practice of mantra repetition.

The Divine Presence is within and without. A mantra is the Divine Presence as a sound. Your personal mantra of choice may be better found from a knowledgeable guru, but this is not always true.

Repeat your mantra every second, or every moment, or every micro moment, or as much as possible. (Or throw away this booklet – if it's not for you at this time!).

If you don't have a mantra, choose one of these.

Firstly - Om Guru Om
Hari Om
Soham
Hare Krishna
Om Namah Shivaya

There are many, many, more.

Mantra purpose

One key purpose of mantra energy is to bypass depression or other mental stumbling blocks. Because you bypass it, there is then a cure or a remedy for low mood, negative perception and depleted energy. You are in your *Higher Rooms* where the light leaves behind the darkness. It's a refuge and a "go to" for any problem, and it alleviates the need for "running away". A mantra's power is very interesting because it's the distilled sound of *Life and the Universe.* (My term for "everything"). It's not just being Transcendental. It's that, and connection to any experience, no matter what. You become Transcendental in your spiritual approach to life first, and then you also swap darkness for light – the Guru function. As your True Enlightened Self you also become the Guru. Then......?

You can use mantra power for anything, including destructive goals or objectives. It will do the work for you that you desire. (I.e. can be used for wealth or spiritual growth as per your choice). It's a bit like nuclear energy. It's a vibrational energy that can heal or destroy.

Its real use though is to connect the soul via mind, body, and your environment, to allow understanding of positive and negative experiences as aligned with a spiritual awareness. This is when you understand Kali Yuga – the age of destruction, or the "dark age". This is the world we are in. Lots of wars, famines, and suffering on a global scale. The Hindus and Buddhists understand this, and worship Kali, the fierce goddess of destruction. She is pictured holding severed heads. This world will sever our ego, metaphorically depicted as the heads that Kali is holding, because as person realizes that "all life is suffering", this becomes one's realization. Then we will want to transcend it all. We will accept our Guru, who is our self and not really separate. The Guru is the True Self I want to be. The gurus and teachers are voices within and without, but really neither. (Not voices in the sense of psychosis experiences). These voices will speak as you move away from seeing the world as playground for desire satisfaction, and more of a learning place to enable realization of the True Self. They will seem to come to you but are already present in you. Then a mantra's higher vibration rises us above darkness, or even evil forces. Mantras create a shield of "armour" to protect from curses, violence and accidents. (So, devotees paradoxically also pray to the "violent" Kali to get protection from violence). Some mantras have aggressive or destructive vibrations, so in contradiction they should be used for protection only – to achieve a peaceful environment.

There is a view that the chanting of mantras is a practice to help focus the mind.
However, this view is a very partial perspective.

Divine Grace Yoga - Mantra Shakti

A mantra of any power exists in a totally different dimension to the mind.

It is a syllable, word, and sound that relates to a particular state of consciousness that, whilst related to mind, (and body), emanates from a soul or spirit source. For instance, to use the word Guru as a mantra, is to identify on a subtle plane with the role of the Guru, which is to lead from darkness to light, from ignorance to knowledge, (in a spiritual sense).

Gu & *Ru*, combined with Om, which is the spiritual word for and sound of the Universe, the mantra then both identifies and takes the user from darkness to light, or to the universe centre.

The practitioner, (who repeats or chants the mantra), becomes immersed in a sense of being at the centre of all life & light. Thus, to meditate with this mantra, the best effect occurs with visualization of journeying out of the body, beyond the city, the country, the solar system, the galaxy, and so forth. (A continuation would be that of ascending to the Cosmic Centre).

Then what happens?

Samadhi

This position at or within this Centre is the deepest form of meditation, (called *Samadhi*), with regard to external meditation on this aspect of the Divine.

However, to think that human consciousness then cannot exist is not quite correct.

For instance, in deep sleep, it seems that the individual does not exist, yet on awakening all awareness comes back again.

In a further development of the Samadhi state the seeker needs then to find the Centre within the human "heart", which is not the physical one.

The universe in its essential Divine essence then becomes more entwined in the seekers' experience of human life.

Then awareness of Divinity, God or Higher Power, can become a stronger component of daily life experience.

The Heart mantras

Om will still remain as the supreme mantra, as it encompasses all - external, internal, & beyond.

Then one can add an *Ishta* Mantra - this is your chosen sound manifestation or representation of your Divinity. (Your *Ishta* or Lord).

For example, Hindu derived mantras are such as *Krisna, Rama,* or *Hari*.

Other religions also have a range of mantras.

Divine in the body

Divine Grace Yoga - Mantra Shakti

A problem that seems to be common in spiritual seeking is the issue of the bodily and mental needs, desires, and the gamut of the human condition.
Many aspects of religion, (& spiritual practice), have sought to somehow separate out the body/mind, disregard it, discipline it fiercely, or somehow transcend it all.
This seems to lead to endless struggle.
Therefore, the next step in the use of mantras is to seek incorporation of the body/mind into spiritual practices, and hence incorporation into the Divinity that is both within and external – no separation.
Certain mantras can be used for this step.
At this point it could be useful to do some reading on spiritual forces & healing forces within the body.
Knowledge about the chakras & Kundalini is one place to start.
The purpose of spiritual practice, which unites the human forces or sublimates them, is to attain a harmonious loop of the human and the Divine - where human nature is not an obstacle, (or even "evil")
This practice where the merger of divine and human is sought is *Tantric practice.*
Tantric practice recognizes the whole gamut of human emotion & nature, (but seeks to move to a higher level of being without denying human activity, such as sex).

Divine Grace Yoga – Mantra Shakti

Mantras – long-term perspective

If one takes the time to study this topic in some depth, one will find that there is a wealth of information and in-depth science of the power of a word. Each mantra from the ancient historical past of India has an author - a wise sage. It has a supernatural being that informs that transcendental component. It has an underlying – long term seed form, which is the subtle unconscious power of that sound. The sound itself is allied to a particular energy, (Shakti), which is the unseen vibration of that sound. This is somewhat similar to sound waves which can be heard when channeled through an instrument, (such as a radio). All of these components are held together by an unseen pillar or pin. (Just like the body held upright by the spine). The mantra, however, must be awakened through its use by the person using it. So, a mantra could be merely supplementary to other spiritual practices, or vice versa. However, the mantra can be used as the key practice spiritually and also to achieve any other outcome that is sought. Sound produces forms through its vibrations, and the repetition of a particular mantra brings forth awareness of both the form that is meditated on and the purification that is sought. Logically any person using a mantra would want to use one that represents a favored deity, or materialistic outcome. The choice of form of one's Deity or desired outcome, becomes one's choice of mantra.

The mantra can also be a refuge. Its repetition can allow release or escape from certain difficult mental problems or thoughts, and move the minds focus to a healthier location. Constant repetition over a long period can enable a shift from a deep-seated negative personal perspective towards the higher planes of light and energy.

The mantra is of course a spiritual word, although you may hear that any repeated word has its own power. Logically, it does not make sense to repeat some obnoxious phrases. For instance, whilst eating dinner certain words could provoke unpleasant regurgitation! Logically it makes sense to repeat something sweet, light, and healthy -unless one has a death wish!

Types of mantras

Om is well-known by many across the world. It is considered, however, by some teachers to be a mantra more suited for those of a monastic inclination. Other mantras are the names of ones preferred Deity. There is a plethora of mantras in Buddhism, untold numbers in Hinduism, and under a different schema many such uses of sacred words in other religions.

Divine Grace Yoga - Mantra Shakti

OM is considered to be the most important mantra, and longer mantras generally begin with OM.

It is a seed mantra. Other seed mantras can also be considered to be Goddess mantras, and they are part of the Tantric tradition. They are themselves a core element of Tantric practice.

Tue it is considered by many teachers, that a mantra should be imparted by someone who has a teacher role, or specific knowledge and wisdom of this area.

Certainly, mantras have been taken up from books, from inner intuition, by divine initiation (nonphysical teacher or deity), or by other means.

The seed mantras including Om are considered to be powerful & therefore more suitable to practitioners initiated into the wider lore of Yoga, Vedanta, and Tantra.

It is the repetition and practice that is most important. Therefore, alongside practice, and awareness & knowledge about use of mantras will help to ensure better outcomes.

It is deemed helpful to do repetition at a quiet time such as dusk or drawn, sitting in a quiet and comfortable place, using a good posture, and a distraction free environment. One can also use a rosary, (*Mala*), keep a log or count, use verbal or mental repetition, or even write.

Divine Grace Yoga - Mantra Shakti

Japa

Repetition is called Japa, and this is what you want to be doing for Enlightenment Now.

Choose your mantra.

Do the Japa.

Then more questions may arise following the practice of Japa.

A mantra can be "tailor made" for the individual or may change as practice progress is.

Multiple mantras can be used as some mantras are prayers. They are "extended" mantras, and a longer prayer may proceed then repetition of a short mantra, (such as a seed mantra).

A Guru or Teacher at this point will be very useful!

Techniques

- Repeat the mantra anywhere, any time.
- Use quiet time when possible.
- Sit cross-legged at times if possible.
- Early morning is "prime time".
- Use a Mala or rosary when possible.

Chapter 2

Kundalini & Shakti

Kundalini

Otherwise known as the serpent power, Kundalini is considered to be like a coiled snake of energy at the base of the spine when dormant. When awakened, it arises in a sinuous movement through the center of the spine to the crown of the head, through the chakras. Kundalini arises in a sinuous movement through the centre of the spine to the crown of the head. Along the way are centres of energy called chakras and each one of those chakras has specific and particular attributes. As mentioned, some consider that the Kundalini rises up from the sleeping coiled state only when awakened through yogic practices, or by the special grace of a teacher who obviously has the powers, (*Siddhis*), to make this happen. Some practitioners say that a highly developed spiritual person has naturally free-flowing energies, and the Kundalini rises up through all the chakras & freely moves past the crown chakra into the sacred ether to a transcendental state. Then the energy of the divine being or the higher power revolves back down into the body, purifying all the centres. Some yogis will practice activities to make controlled & channelled energy rise up through the chakras, using meditation on the chakras centre, whilst using mantras to purify each location. Kundalini can therefore be moved as a continuous flow upwards as well as downwards, free flowing without blockage.

What does not come so easily is the inside knowledge about the workings of Kundalini and Shakti, with the use of sacred sounds including seed mantras. (A Siddha will know the secret: the inside knowledge of the area and will know how certain sounds go with certain chakras, or work in certain ways to develop one's ability to both function in the world and to transcend it). Getting the free flow of Kundalini may be considered by some to be relatively easy, but this does not of itself guarantee that a practitioner is freed from many years of struggle. It is here and now in the body, in the daily grind of life business that the work still occurs. Not just to survive or then flourish in human terms, but also to have a human ability to be a spiritual soul rather than just a physically embodied one.

When the practitioner freely moves energy up & down through the chakras with true purification, it becomes easier to focus & be on the higher levels. At that point the locus of meditation can become the heart, and the higher centres become a route through which divine energy revolves, descends and moves out to others. At this point other mantras & meditations may be preferred by the practitioner.

The use of specific seed mantras may speed up true purification & achievement of the higher levels.

Kundalini awakening

The contentious issue regarding Kundalini is "side effects of Kundalini awakening". Historically, Kundalini Yoga is approached via a Guru. An experienced guru can awaken this "sleeping serpent" in another person through "transfer of energy". In our modern world this might not be feasible or practical, given the nature of this dark era (Kali Yuga). It may not be possible to get a guru who can assist Kundalini awakening.

It is necessary now to offer this "secret" inner process as an option for any practitioner, desiring to awaken Kundalini for spiritual progress. Guidance also comes from the Inner Guru, which can be accessed to get "initiation" and awakening. Kundalini awakening has been described as risky when there is no clarity of use. This is because the chakras get activated & accessed. (See diagram of chakras in the appendix

Divine Grace Yoga – Mantra Shakti

section also). Theoretically all sorts of negative materials are then released on the way to the Crown Chakra. Even so this Kundalini awakening is an important requirement for this *Om Divine Grace Yoga* pathway and can be understood with right guidance. I have given information and instruction on this topic. Also, as a result of receiving the Divine Guidance from within there will be appropriate additional clarity. (This can be accessed via surrender to ones chosen deity – for instance). Good intent and practice is required for good results. Access the Divine Guidance via Divine Grace may be from within or without. Then there will be appropriate additional clarity.

More Kundalini information

Does is a rising and hence awakening of Kundalini, and the descending of Divine Energy really awakens consciousness in the body? This is in direct conflict with some described aspects of practice, where Kundalini is seen as only rising up and then out of the Crown Chakra. It is true that ultimately the purpose and function of kundalini awakening is finally an enabling of an experience of the *witness* stage, where we see through life and see it *as it really is*. The kundalini is a holy force aligned to the Goddess energy or Shakti. It takes us out of our material craziness, but also it takes us through them, not passing by them or burying

Divine Grace Yoga - Mantra Shakti

them. The Awakening does not make us mad or bad, we already were!

We do however have to take what cure we really need to take and leave behind what we can discard. For instance, much of religion has become distorted over the years, and often serves no purpose, or confuses and even destroys us. We need then to see religion as something that may help us only in parts. If it's really "the full ticket" then you don't need this book!

Does Prozac have a place? Does Valium have a place? Do we get a therapist? Herbalist, crystal gazer, acupuncturist, psychiatrist, hypnotist? The options are multiple, but the opinions are even more than you can imagine. Some believe psychiatry is the work of the Devil. For some it's the New Age. In short, degrees of fundamentalism are very common. It is actually all around us in many forms and even is the new norm! Others are fanatic about their beliefs which are the "be all & end all". The *Om Divine Grace Yoga* should be seen as one option amongst many, with no importance attached unless it works for you!

Kundalini yoga is supposed to be therapeutic. There is some research into its practice. Of course, quite a lot of research looks at the value of meditation. Writers in this field have expressed views that the Kundalini process can include some generation of physical and mental problems. Others agree that the Kundalini process can lead to the unveiling of the true self and enlightenment. The Kundalini awakening can set off: writhing, dancing, emotional distress/euphoria, various physical/mental symptoms etc. (Got to put the side effects on the box these days!). It after all a cleansing process!

Depression may be located in the heart chakra, but its effects appear to be in more focused the brain area. The right side of the heart is described as a true spiritual centre. A number of teachers are very clear on this view. Depression also has echoes in monasticism and renunciation. The Sanskrit word *vairagya* means dispassion. In this case, it is almost a complete abhorrence of the world that drives a person into the state of renunciation known as *Sannyasa.* This can be seen as similar to the state of *Anhedonia*, which is in psychiatry is a loss of interest in all the world that previously appeared attractive to oneself. The early life of the Buddha also illustrates this overwhelming urge through "sadness", to remove oneself from the world at all costs, even if he was a king before he left the palace. One view would be that he had a very low mood and was experiencing a crisis of depressive disorder! (The correlation with mood etc. has been explores in my previous books).

Divine Grace Yoga - Mantra Shakti

The connection between the centres of the heart and the right side of the body is an esoteric subject all of its own. The product of being spiritually soul located between these two areas, may be a conflict between this life of the family, society and the male/female domain, and the domain of monasticism, and introspection. It is cave vs the cafe! Alternatively, we could see here also, a focus on good vs evil. This heart is perhaps the "primary" chakra rather than the crown chakra, as it is more than just the one chakra. It also seems to be an area that is reached, or rather returned to, after the crown chakra has been breached. A sort of umbrella of light moves down from the crown chakra to the heart area, which is situated all around the body, but with a focus slightly to the right of the heart.

The concept of depression, (or other mental health topics), and relevance to Kundalini and spiritual awakening, can be seen as a higher process that is trying to connect and balance both of flow and of energy to and from divine consciousness. This meets the needs and aspirations of the spiritual practitioner. Also, in present society that is moving into ever advancing research, approaches to treatment of mental health problems may come to a recognition of Kundalini type "electricity". If currently medication approaches stay limited in their effectiveness, it needs be that the true workings of the brain are found, and the consequent cures thus "discovered". Kundalini may be seen then to help, (scientifically), with mental wellbeing.

Shakti

Shakti is also considered to be the universal energy or Goddess energy, the creative force of the Divine. In one sense the masculine aspect is the transcendental, and the female is the creation. It does depend on which school of thought of philosophy one reads. For some there is only one unified being, and the world is *Maya* - illusion. Those who are devotees of the Goddess see the journey within the manifested world as the way to liberation or higher consciousness. This does involve partaking of all the world offers. This is the true meaning of Tantra, the spiritual acceptance of the external reality, and all its temptations. (And of course, it's suffering)!

Other yoga paths are *Gyana, Bhakti, Karma, Raja Yoga*. (The yoga paths of Knowledge, Devotion, Service. Plus, the "King" path of Raja Yoga).

The contentious issue regarding Shakti is: are you ready for a female God! Historically, Shakti Yoga is approached via a Guru for initiation and guidance. In our modern world this might not be feasible or practical, given the nature of this dark era (Kali Yuga). It may not be possible to get a guru who can assist you in this area.

It is necessary now to offer this spiritual pathway and process as an option for any practitioner, desiring to connect with Shakti for spiritual progress. Guidance also comes from the Inner Guru, which can be accessed to get "initiation" and awakening. This Shakti component is an important requirement for this *Om Divine Grace Yoga* pathway and can be understood with right guidance. I have written information and instructions on this topic, but there are many other perspectives to be found. Also, as a result of receiving the Divine Guidance from within, (the inner guru), and other instruction, there will be appropriate additional clarity. (This guidance can also be accessed via surrender to ones chosen Deity). Good intent and practice are required for good results.

Shakti information

Shakti is the third component of *Om Divine Grace Yoga and* is also considered to be the universal energy or Goddess energy - the creation force of the divine being.

In this sense the masculine aspect of divine being is seen as a transcendental power which is beyond form and shape & the female aspect is seen as the external creation. When practitioners worship the Shakti or Goddess form, they can worship the divine being as the world, the universe, or creation.

Some schools of thought and philosophy accept only one monotheistic divinity. Those with an interest in Kundalini and Shakti view the female aspects as either continuous with the male transcendent consciousness, or as coexisting. Religious belief is of course to be recognised in this dimension. In the *Vedanta* philosophy, there is only one unified Divine Being and creation is sometimes called Maya. Maya represents as an illusory universe. This is in the sense of illusion as being something to be transcended, or even avoided, in order to realise that Divine Consciousness and Ultimate Truth, (as per *Vedanta* philosophy). In this case only the transcendental locus has truth. Vedanta means: "the end part of the Vedas" and was developed after a swing away from ritualistic practice in ancient Indian times.

For those who are devotees of the Goddess, manifested Shakti is the way of liberation or achievement of higher consciousness. It involves partaking of all that the world offers, even though the final goal is liberation and freedom from birth and death, (or rebirth). Such practitioners are called *Shaktas* - the worshippers of Shakti or the Goddess. The path is also the Tantric path because the Tantric path is simply spirituality with full acceptance of the world and one's place in it as a human being. As a Tantric practitioner the whole gamut of desires, needs, & goal focused activities etc., is seen as needing to be both understood as well as transcended. Kundalini is involved in both the Tantric focus as well as the practices of a Siddha, or "perfected yogi", because a Siddha will have ability, control, and knowledge regarding the Kundalini, the nature of desire and involvement in the world, and the way through, (using the world), to a higher spirituality. Whatever practice chosen, the reality for most is that the road of spiritual practice can be a lengthy one, with a lot of repetition, endeavour and discipline. It may be possible to get to one's goal of connection with God, (or Goddess), in one hit as in becoming "born-again", and then move on from this life into a permanent spiritual space, such as that one called *Heaven*. For others it may take many revolving lifetimes of practice to truly achieve liberation from the cycle of birth and death. Either way simply believing one is in enlightened, or in touch completely with one's highest Divinity, may not be an actual reality. Some of those professing such perfection seem to have not been able to overcome or manage some basic common human frailties. The way of the Tantric practitioner or the worshipper of the Goddess energy, is to accept the human nature and work with it, not against it, until it there is true proof of purification, where the practitioner sits in a natural spiritual state of bliss and knowledge. (Not a "perfect human" however). This state is one of embodiment in *Sat Chit Ananda*, (Existence, Knowledge, Bliss).

It's God and Goddess in amalgamation for me. Thus, I do not subscribe to the patriarchal religious precepts which came from our patriarchal history. Time has moved on and society seems to be moving on from a God, who is some guy with a beard sitting up in the clouds. The Goddess, and her energy or Shakti, is quite prominent in Hindu systems, but historically also did not take centre stage. There is more widespread leaning to Shakti devotion with regard to Tantric Buddhism, primarily from Tibet. We are comprised of male and female elements or personalities and this ratio does vary. Hormones may drive us as humans, but do they affect our religious preferences? I don't know of any scientific research on this topic. Either way, when one is in touch with one's inner guru, then it will all come clear, and the dilemmas regarding what to do with our spiritual or religious practice will evaporate.

Shakti and other spiritual pathways

There is a pathway of knowledge known as *Gyana* Yoga. This in its purest form entails holding a philosophy that "I am Cosmic Consciousness". (In individualized form). My essence is then the same as the essence of the Divine. I just have to let go of the covering of Maya, or my ego-based identification. Follow this approach then through the teachings of Vedanta.

There are however variations of Vedanta that are not pure monism, nor seemingly allied to Gnosticism. Then it is all Divine still, but the philosophy diverges to say that I am an individual always and will only be separate from my God or Deity – not absorbed. Separate, in other words, for eternity. This is when there is worship of a separate Deity, a Krishna, a Jesus, or Buddha. (Although the Buddha taught differently, many worship him as their Deity and are on the path of devotion).

Divine Grace Yoga – Mantra Shakti

Then we have other yogas. "Kingly" or Raja Yoga, is based on doing a lot of mediation and getting to Samadhi, the divine self-realized meditation goal and state. It's a bit similar to what the Buddhist meditators are seeking, especially in the Westernized versions of practice. The differences are deep & internal philosophy based, but I have found that my meditation experience is much the same, whatever group I am sitting in.

Next, we have Kundalini Yoga which is allied to the Siddha, or the "perfected guru" pathway, which in turn is allied to Shakti, (Goddess Energy), elements. Siddhi means essentially "powers", referring to a variety of powers that can be attained through advanced yogic meditation practice. Shakti also means power, but it is the essential nature of the female form or aspect of the Divine. Complicated, especially as I present a simplified view, possibly seen as "flawed" by some adherents of specific practices! My apologies to those who know the in-depth true story! Or those who disagree significantly! The idea of Kundalini Yoga is that it takes the Shakti energy and places it in the body as segments of differentiated energy. It's all Shakti, but comes in different expressions, just as the Goddess appears as Tara Devi, Durga, Saraswati etc.

Divine Grace Yoga - Mantra Shakti

The segments of differentiated energy form are in chakra such as the brow, heart navel etc. Thus, Kundalini works up and down in the body through the chakras. It flows through a spinal channel (or channels) and signifies that the whole body is a spiritual entity. It works on physical, psychological, mental, and emotional levels. Everything. Connected to the neurochemical/electrical activities of the nervous system, but on a different plane. Different planes are ok for the scientifically minded. It's quantum physics, right?

At some point the full process of energy involvement through the chakras becomes a transcendental experience. This is because the chakras and Kundalini are in essence spiritual energies that seem to be associated bodily but are only thus for the purpose of temporal engagement. The ego becomes refined, and then as the crown or topmost chakra is reached, Kundalini is revealed as a Divine transcendent energy. It is free to flow, and can cascade around the body, especially to the outer ring round the chest area. This is synonymous with a deep spiritual awareness, and a connection with the Divine Goddess energy seated out of and to the right of the heart. It is for me in the form of *Tara Devi* but takes the form the individual requires. (Depending on what healing/guiding mixture is needed). In the broadest sense there is an innate attainment of Bliss. We can still enjoy our cappuccinos, and what's shown in the movies, but it is very much a practical experience of being a witness to our participation in life. It's just the *Prarabdha that is then left.* Prarabdha is a Sanskrit word for the accumulated forces of karma. Like a train running on after it's no longer got fuel. From a religious perspective, we worship a Deity firstly as external deity, and as a powerful being, but then remember that we are already in Oneness, connected to the Divine, because we are already part of that. Then we cease to be "doers" as that part is surrendered to a God or Deities. Then also we can realize our true nature in the sense that a spark is not different in essence to the fire.

In Tibetan Buddhism there is worship of Deities such as Tara Devi. She appears as a female bodhisattva in Mahayana Buddhism, and as a female Buddha in Vajrayana Buddhism. She is known as the "mother of liberation", as a savior who liberates souls from suffering, and represents the virtues of success in work and achievements. Hinduism in particular lays out all the religious, spiritual, and philosophical options like a

Divine Grace Yoga - Mantra Shakti

smorgasbord. Take your pick and, in today's secular world, mix and mingle. (In the past and today in some countries, such an approach was/is considered blasphemous!). You can also choose your gurus or, "swap around". Please debate!

Shakti is the third section/component of *Om Divine Grace Yoga.* Shakti is also considered to be the universal energy or Goddess energy - the creation force of the divine being.

Shakti arises in a sinuous movement through the centre of the spine to the crown of the head. Along the way are centres of energy called chakras and each one of those chakras has specific and particular attributes. As mentioned, some consider that the Kundalini rises up from the sleeping coiled state only when awakened through yogic practices, or by the special grace of a teacher who obviously has the powers, (Siddhis), to make this happen. Some practitioners say that a highly developed spiritual person has naturally free-flowing energies, and the kundalini rises up through all the chakras & freely moves past the crown chakra into the sacred ether to a transcendental state. Then the energy of the divine being or the higher power revolves back down into the body, purifying all the centres. Some yogis will practice activities to make controlled &

channelled energy rise up through the chakras, using meditation on the chakras centre, whilst using mantras to purify each location. Kundalini can therefore be moved as a continuous flow upwards as well as downwards, free flowing without blockage.

What does not come so easily is the inside knowledge about the workings of Kundalini and Shakti, with the use of sacred sounds including seed mantras. (A Siddha will know the secret: the inside knowledge of the area and will know how certain sounds go with certain chakras, or work in certain ways to develop one's ability to both function in the world and to transcend it). Getting the free flow of Kundalini may be considered by some to be relatively easy, but this does not of itself guarantee that a practitioner is freed from many years of struggle. It is here and now in the body, in the daily grind of life business that the work still occurs. Not just to survive or then flourish in human terms, but also to have a human ability to be a spiritual soul rather than just a physically embodied one.
When the practitioner freely moves energy up & down through the chakras with true purification, it becomes easier to focus & be on the higher levels. At that point the locus of meditation can become the heart, and the higher centres become a route through which divine

energy revolves, descends and moves out to others. At this point other mantras & meditations may be preferred by the practitioner.

The use of specific seed mantras may speed up true purification & achievement of the higher levels.

Shakti is therefore a main component of *Om Divine Grace Yoga* because Shakti is also considered to be the universal energy or Goddess energy - the creation force of the Divine Being.

Goddess Power – a summary

The Goddess represents both Maya in the whole world of human suffering, searching and pleasure seeking, and also represents the link back to the Universal Being, which is formless, pervasive Cosmic Consciousness. (Some people call it God). The Goddess is the energy or Shakti represented by the Kundalini force, which rises up the spine with the human awakening, to break through at the crown of the head, so as to allow the liberation of the soul.

The Goddess is also the focus of the Tantric way that includes the world in worship. Instead of exclusion, there is inclusion of "money, food and sex". (Which is in humans often in need of being dealt without addictions/compulsions). The Goddess is the link or a means of transferring human identity to Divine identity, by generating the understanding of what Enlightenment is about.

Bypass all spiritual practice hype & confusion, by a surrendering process. That is to leave it up to the Goddess or rather give it over to the Goddess. This can be replicated of course in whatever one's pathway or religion is. It is irrelevant, get on with the job, and attain Enlightenment and Realization.

To have the best of both, (or all), worlds, combine both a personal deity with an impersonal deity, and some "scientific" practice of working with bodily centers using the Yogas of meditation, mantra and yoga postures. As well as a focus on chakra energies to connect the mental & physical body to the Shakti energy. This may seem at times a contradictory pathway but has been in practice from ancient times as per the writing of the sages and seers. They espoused lofty monistic philosophies about a formless consciousness as Ultimate Reality but also worshiped their chosen or Ishta Deity. (Devi, Rama, Shiva etc.).

The mantras though are the key activity, and these

refer to specific goddess forms, (of the one Divine Shakti). As they are directed to specific chakras in the body, this repetition of mantras purifies and brings light to the human realm. They also work subtly on mental health issues, addictions and obsessions.

The work of the Divine Goddess is about spinning us into the web of Maya, seemingly on the surface. Then to trip us into mundane activities, but really to eventually liberate, because the Divines works happen in the world, and not in some cave or monastery!

The Divine is perfect and complete, and emanations from the Divine, such as this world of *Life and the Universe*, are complete in purpose, though it all seems crazy from a disturbed mind perspective. Be it your belief in the Goddess as the creatrix, or God as Him, or as the Big Bang. Whatever is produced in this Cosmic Consciousness is interconnected with sound. Therefore, the mantra will heal the craziness and allow different perspectives. It can seem very slow, especially if you are feeling some agitation. Remember though, you are not your body and mind. You are the "witness". Your natural state is *Sat, Chit, Ananda.* - Existence, Knowledge, Bliss.

Divine Grace Yoga - Mantra Shakti

Truth is the "I" of you as the Divine Soul. It is your birth right. You may need to connect with it, (it seems), even though it is just *there*. You have to sit on your mountain, (of solid spiritual practice), and chant the mantra through the time of the dark clouds and the storms.

We may separate ourselves from Light, and then we live in darkness. Change perspective and focus at this point or suffer the consequences.
Seek Divine Grace. The Light will shine through, and with it the Divine Sound will manifest.
Our consciousness identifies with matter as ego, and the illusion that is Maya, gets created, but also can be destroyed eventually. Nothing really disappears, because nothing really appears – illusory stuff all of it. We can agree or disagree with much of science, as per choice, but the Big Bang is after all a "large sound'. It's just mind perspectives still, and not so relevant in the state of Enlightenment. Confused views of science. (A very young development), are not the position of the Transcendental Self. However, we are in fear, and rush around, because we cannot find ourselves experiencing *being* the Transcendent Self, and cannot truly see the un-reality of the Maya created forms in life. We do not connect with the underlying sound then. The mantra

makes this connection, and tales us to the point of Enlightenment (Mantra repetition may seem to be a somewhat artificially initially). Finally, Maya is seen as just the Goddess going about her business!

Chapter 3
The *Siddha* & Divine Grace

Siddha Yoga

I have written about the topic of the Siddha in my previous books. This is a much-revised version of that material with additional commentary and guidance. It is designed to enable practical use by a spiritual practitioner interested in this pathway.

The contentious issue regarding the Siddha is: are you ready for a Guru who will make you change one way or another? Historically, this pathway is approached via a Sat Guru for initiation and guidance. In our modern world this might not be feasible or practical, given the nature of this dark era (Kali Yuga). It may not be possible to get a guru who can assist you in this area. Guidance can also come from the Inner Guru, which can be accessed to get "initiation" and awakening. This Siddha component is an important requirement for this *Om Divine Grace Yoga* pathway and can be understood with right guidance. The Guru transmission can come via inner as well as external directions. When such guidance is received, there will be additional clarity about one's spiritual direction. If Divine Grace from the Sat Guru is obtained the possibilities are endless! (This guidance can also be accessed via surrender to one's chosen personal Deity).

What is a Siddha Yogi?

A yogi can be a renunciate monk a person who has renounced the world and become celibate. It can also be anybody! (Who does the required practice). This may in India be a *Swami*, who is usually a celibate monk. Swami literally means someone who has transcended the ego – *swa* (give up or surrender), *& mi* (myself). So, *s*wami *is* really about a person's attributes and not what color cloth they wear. Traditionally a swami wears ochre red or similar color robes, signifying a body and mind that is being "burnt up" by the fire of renunciation. So, color is important up to a point. What color car do you prefer? More importantly what is your favorite color & how do you use it?

The word Siddha means *a perfected being* and *one with spiritual powers*. Therefore, the Siddha is one who is a spiritually enlightened being with sufficient power or abilities to enable the transformation of others, and not one who has merely attained some personal yogic state or power. (Nor a swami).

A true guru is a true teacher – a Sat Guru. A Perfected Teacher, who is a Divine being is one who has reached the state of oneness with the Divinity, (sometimes known as God).

Some see this sort of human as a being who is an incarnation, or *Avatar*, when God becomes human. Thus, people may worship such a human, who appears as a Divine representation. This may be Jesus or the Buddha, or one's own Sat Guru. Such a one is in the state of *Nirvana*. Nirvana or Moksha is a state of both enlightenment and freedom, (from birth and death). A Guru does not however need to be an Avatar. A Guru can also be perceived as a human being made perfect by his/her own endeavor. They are seen as their own teacher; of whatever spiritual path or religion they have chosen. (These views and other viewpoints may be subject to your own logical view and are the subject of much debate in some circles. Also, leaders of some sects may be highly negative about the spiritual "credentials" of other teachers. Competition!

Divine Grace Yoga - Mantra Shakti

In India there are many holy persons who practice austerity and penance, meditate and follow a variety of spiritual paths, while garbed as a swami, or holy person. There are quite a few who are seen as Siddhas by their devotees, and a number who have a large international following. Some attain the Supreme Goal and become perfected, in the eyes of their followers, without necessarily presenting themselves in a monastic role or environment. They are considered perfected in the eyes of their adherents, whatever religion, country, and role they manifest in and are present in.

All such beings, (if they are not in it for the money & power), can teach humanity to be, not just "ordinary", but also to themselves strive to attain the same place where they sit. A place where there is a Divine state of awareness.
Siddhas should teach, (in my opinion), that any of us can and should attain a state of spiritual perfection whilst remaining in the human condition.

The caveat is that the Siddha is more than any human role. Therefore, the soul that has that Siddha power and ability is in the enlightened domain, and does not really need to follow the typical practice or external presentation of a monastic practitioner. Free to do anything?

One who has achieved that state quite naturally is in renunciation mode and is not swayed by the external world- particularly by desire, greed and lust. Therefore, that soul does not need to wear red, as the fire burns fiercely inside.
He or she can be in any predicament or situation, or country or lifestyle, or role in the external world.

The Siddha being transcends the external world, which is seen as Maya. The Sanskrit word Maya means illusory, transient or temporary, in terms of the world which is a place of delusion and dream.

However, the Siddha is like a swan on the water floating and staying dry. In Sanskrit this is known as Paramhamsa (Great =*Param*, Swan = *Hansa*). In mythology the Paramhansa can also separate milk from water. Also is one who's in the world but not in the world - just floating on and above it. Still a human being, but with a certain super spiritual attainment. This does not deny the reality that the person who achieves this may have been previously a so-called "ordinary" human being and is also one who still has the potential to present as an ordinary human being. (May go unnoticed and unappreciated).

It is considered in Hinduism that the human birth is the place where one has potential to achieve what is called Nirvana or Moksha, and thus the final birth - with freedom from the bondage of endless cycles of birth and death.
This human life thus has spiritual meaning when used for all endeavors that led to transcendence the human condition. Thus, humanistic service orientated endeavors are also seen as uplifting and beneficial.

Other religions, even if not acknowledging or agreeing with this philosophy and perspective, still exhort us to use our lifespan for spiritual and religious purpose.
A born-again person is deemed to have rebirth into a spiritual world, whilst still experiencing and journeying through the physical and mental spheres.
There are of course certain activities and practices that have to be followed if one is to attain the highest spiritual goal whilst travelling in the world. Spiritual endeavor and practice are required. There are also certain conditions and circumstances that are required to achieve progress on the spiritual path

Divine Grace Yoga - Mantra Shakti

This way of *Mantra Shakyi Yoga* described is based on *Siddha Yoga, Tantric Yoga, Kundalini Yoga, Mantra Yoga*, plus other western and eastern religious and spiritual practices. Plus, the worship of a personal deity or Goddess/God, and the realities of life experience in the human world. (*Life and the Universe*).

This is also a personalized summary, provided to assist any person on the spiritual path where possible. There are also many texts books and sources of information available to anyone who wishes to study in depth the topics touched on. Therefore, I am essentially describing my own spiritual adventure and progress, in terms of what I have experienced studied and learnt. Everyone's journey will be different, and I make no claim to having the "right path".

This structured written continuation of all these themes are here to assist with the seeking and practicing the path towards one's own spiritual goals.

The Components of Siddha Yoga

One
A guru - the true guru or Sat Guru
A human connection is usually needed to facilitate easy access to the Divine, (as the inner soul or the external

deity), and the true guru manifests energy by grace. This enables the journey to proceed. For some this guru is the teacher who is recognized as an Incarnation first and human second.

For others this being is someone who is still here foremost as a human, albeit Realized. One whom they can follow and receive instruction from. For others an amalgamation of a number of teachers is experienced. For others guidance comes from within - an inner teacher or a force that seems to be external. The Siddha embodies a human based form of Divinity, but some will talk to God or other "angelic" or similar manifestation through an Inner Voice mechanism. This may do the work of Guru and guidance for that individual.

The guru is "one who dispels darkness", which is the center core function of a Siddha
Maybe not totally, or maybe in some areas, (in the case of a "partial" Siddha with power and ability to a limited extent), the energy sought will be that which is needed for the guidance of the individual at a particular time.

Therefore, there may be several teachers who each guide in their own specific and special way. There is always a lineage of some sort except in the case of exceptional teachers who seem to materialize out of nowhere for the sake of the century, or multiple centuries.

Either way or whatever the scenario, turning a human to the Divine makes the guide process work so much more spontaneously and effectively. If the one who seeks has an understanding of the guru function and purpose, then the Divine or Divine perfection, Siddhi powers will "intervene". Even for material gain, (if one seeks this), as all developments are more accessible with the receipt of the guru's Grace. This grace dispels "darkness", negativity, "stuckness", and even gloom and despair.
Even if you want to learn a trade, get a degree or make some money, there is always a need to get a guide/teacher to help get you there.

Two

In the path of the Siddha there is a need to understand the spirit force that flows through the body
In the traditional meditation on Kundalini, this energy is seen as coiled at the base of the spine like a serpent, and it arises to pass through the chakras upwards. It arises in a sinuous movement that can cause the

practitioner to feel semi-automatic movements of the body, with an external sinuous "dance" taking place.

This energy known as a form of Shakti, is an energy manifested in the human form, which has significant connection and context with the Goddess powers within.

The awakening of the Kundalini is also connected directly with the Sat Guru, because it is the guru who can bestow *Shakti-Paat*. This is a transmission as a kind of "beaming out" of the guru's power, which awakens another person's kundalini. This is a key Siddhi, (power), of the Siddha guru. With this "power shower" to awaken the source, one can have the Kundalini awakened directly, to rise up through the chakras, and travel beyond the final chakra in the crown of the head.

Otherwise, personal experience of this energy may be problematic, because there may be personal traumatic issues involved in the passage of this energy through the chakras. This personal content may be woken without direction, guidance and oversight.

However, whatever scenario is involved, once practice takes place, the attainment of Divine Realization through Kundalini Yoga still requires full attenuation of awareness, and astute management of the process, to experience the Kundalini energy in only positive and beneficial ways.

Three

In Sanskrit, spiritual practice is called *Sadhana*. This is necessary to enable the practice of going within to flourish. It is also necessary to practice when seeking the Divine force as manifested externally.
There are many views of what God, is or how the Higher Power, the Divine spiritual being, can be attained.
Religions are many, and there are many single or multiple options that are available for the spiritual practitioner to choose from. One needs to not just to choose some way, but to get actively moving along one's chosen path.
Some say you must follow only one path or one way. In reality many people follow different paths at different times in their lives. It does seem logical to keep on one focused way, but then human life is not always logical! People also change their religion!

Divine Grace Yoga - Mantra Shakti

However, what is advisable is to have guide, so that whatever paths/s are taken, they can be followed with some certainty, just as if one has one has a map to read.

It is somewhat similar to treating diseases. The correct medication has to be found, and sometimes it is necessary to change or adjust medication and the dosage. Therefore, it is not uncommon to have more than one spiritual teacher. Or to change or move on from a particular teaching.

So, what is best is what works for you, as long as you do the practice.

Within spiritual practice there is also a need to adopt specific methods that work for each unique individual. One travels paths, but one also uses different means to attain movement. Such as car, a horse, or a camel. What form of meditation or specific type of yoga will you personally adopt? One could ask a similar question in Christianity -will it be Methodist or Catholic or some other?

The traditional path of the *Siddha Marg,* the *following of the perfected being* pathway, has been to use the power of the Kundalini and of mantra sacred word or sounds. In this Dark Age, (Kali Yuga), the repetition of the chosen mantra is deemed to be the easiest way to obtain spiritual power and focus for self-realization.

Japa is repetition of a mantra whereas *dhyana* is meditation on what that mantra means. It is a distilled form of a complex chant or prayer and a simple form that can be repeated at any time silently, mentally, verbally, or even on a subtler level.

Four

A force not often mentioned, is that is that of life experience, as a force that has "power over us". Without life in our experience we do not exist, we do not get to achieve some of our desires, nor do we partake of spiritual paths. Also, human lives seem to present us with lessons and a means to move from gross experience of the body mind to subtler levels. There is a powerful spiritual force behind our life, if we accept the challenge of our problems. That means including mental disorders, addictions, relationships and psychological problems. In other words, the whole gamut of what can seem "just insane". If we deal with life as it is and allow teachers in, we can also move through and find a purposeful momentum or motivation to walk the spiritual path.

Everything can have purpose for our spiritual destiny, even whatever seems bad or desperate. What is seemingly devoid of any credit may also have its purpose or may produce a lesson. Learning about what is painful is a start. Not all knowledge necessarily comes from good things, nor understanding from doing what is right.

The personal journey is a very popular subject and there are many bestsellers in this field. People want to deal with their lives and become happy or at least not be unhappy, sooner or later.
I have written about my own experience of life, especially regarding the connection to going deeper into my spiritual search and practice

In summary the Siddha is a beacon for the path to both God and to perfected development of the human purpose. The Siddha is representative of the divine, and the Siddha path is a way set for us by the lineages and the numbers of Siddhas who have made themselves servants to our spiritual development.

Divine Grace Yoga - Mantra Shakti

This is about life here, but also about transcending it. *Off - floating above the sea of life- the Paramahansa.* The Paramhansa Guru thus is in the world but "untouched" by it. Or this "swan" can separate the cream from the whey - as per mythology!

Divine Grace

Divine Grace is a theological term present in many religions. There is considerable prominence of these two words in Christianity. It has been defined as the Divine influence which operates in humans to regenerate and sanctify, to inspire virtuous impulses, and to impart strength to endure trial and resist temptation, and as an individual virtue or excellence of divine origin. So, how does Divine Grace really work and how do you get it? Well, there are lots of books about Divine Grace. One's personal experience of Divine Grace may be somewhat different, especially if in conflict with the Catholic or Protestant versions or explanations.

In Christianity, *Divine Grace* means a favor of God for humankind. God favors every person, without looking at what they did or how much they are worth. It is the infused presence of God, a presence that is supernatural. Divine Grace is an influence which

Divine Grace Yoga - Mantra Shakti

operates in humans to regenerate, inspire, impart strength to endure trial and resist temptation.

Mantra Shakti Yoga is about faith in the manta and using the mantra can be seen as like a sacrament. You believe, therefore you repeat, and therefore you receive Grace or other effects sought. NB. You need not believe any of this – it's just a religious type of domain. Until you "get the goods", and gets some results, or if it doesn't work, don't do it! Just have the 30-day trial. Sorry - no refunds!

My point is that it is just too easy to get carried away by what has been historically preached or taught. I want to find out what is the Truth behind all religious and spiritual practice and thought, without prejudice. Certainly, without a whiff of any fundamentalism.

My experience of Divine Grace is about my connection with my Goddess, as well as from my Sat Gurus, which is supposedly a Hindu or Buddhist origin philosophical perspective. I have described my search for the Sat Guru in India & beyond in the *Spiritual Journey* section of this book. Also, it's enumerated in more autobiographical detail in *English-Man, Beggar-Man, Holy-Man* and *Divine Grace Journey*. My connectedness to the Goddess in more recent times

Divine Grace Yoga - Mantra Shakti

originates particularly with the *Healing Tara* who is a major Goddess form in Tibetan Buddhism. Now, the how and why of getting to this point doesn't really matter for me, because my need for Divine Grace was born of desperation! Hindu devotional or *bhakti* literature available throughout India and Nepal, is replete with references to Grace as the ultimate key required for spiritual self-realization. The ancient sage *Vashistha* considered it to be the only way to transcend the bondage of lifetimes of karma in this Kali Yuga.

One Hindu philosopher, *Madhavacharya*, held that grace was not a gift from God, but rather must be earned. Grace though, has been defined *as* "God's favor toward the unworthy" or "God's benevolence on the undeserving." Still, the getting of grace requires action, but the action is: "I have to accept grace". Or I have to stop trying to earn grace. Accepting and not striving are very active processes – at least in my experience. Living by grace requires action. Allow ones Higher Power/at Guru/Deity to act and intervene. Release the need to control. Spend more time in prayer and spiritual study.

As previously noted, there is the contrast between seeing Oneness, to perceiving a Deity, which can then be a personal God or Goddess power. The prevailing religious direction has so far primarily been focussed on a patriarchal view of God. Thus, most deities/gods have been male, but in Hinduism and Buddhism there is a variety of choice here. Then there is a considerable body of scripture regarding the Shakti energy as the Goddess power emanation, which is involved individually in the Kundalini and chakras processes. Whatever the philosophical stance, the idea of "who you are", is based on the domain of the bodily based egoic individual, who says, "I am so and so". The universe is then the undivided essence of the Supreme Self, and appearances are like seeing a snake on the ground, when it is just a coil of rope. Consciousness appears then as *Jiva-atman, as* the individual or *Jiva* who feels and thinks, and then does all based on a false perception. In religion though, as discussed, some recognise their separateness to a degree, and then pray to their Deity for the attainment of a kind of oneness, such as residing in heaven alongside ones Deity.

Does then the religious approach take us beyond the cycle of birth and death? (Given that religions are created by human minds from a human perspective – historically also a patriarchal one).

Divine Grace Yoga - Mantra Shakti

Or there is possibly no need for Divine Grace. If we could all achieve Nirvana, salvation, enlightenment, through our own normal natural efforts then we might only need the help of a few teachers.

There is some agreement that as humans we are in some sort of a mess, that we need to get out of this, whether this is seen as be freedom from sin and placement in heaven, or breaking the bonds of ignorance and preventing future reincarnations. Or some other perspective. Most religions seem to have a view that the Divine is actually within, as well as without. Usually, the heart is designated the place for it all to happen.

This view is also the foundation of the Vedanta philosophy, where it is proclaimed that this natural state is what drives the urge to attain salvation. In this philosophy the sinner and the saint, good and bad, rich and poor, are equal in terms of being part of the Cosmic Consciousness, (the *Brahman*), expressed as the individual soul, (the *Atman*).

In summary all religions are clear that we can be saved in some form and get into a kingdom of some form of God enveloped "space" or presence. Again, the essence

Divine Grace Yoga – Mantra Shakti

is within our souls and probably associated with the heart area. This may seem like that is all about being totally self-responsible, and about trying one's best to do good deeds, serve others, and pray to one's Deity. Where from then comes this closely intertwined doctrine of Grace, inseparable from the search and the seeker? Especially when grace seems to render self-responsibility nil and void at times.

Grace is pretty certainly not something that stands out as completely separate, but then again why is it placed sometimes as the ultimate, "out there somewhere". Also, it is fairly often proposed as being the only way to achieve liberation.

The Buddha did not seem to speak much of Divine Grace, whereas in the worlds of other religions, with scriptural announcements about being chosen through Grace seem fairly prominent.

It seems then one can believe that "I have attained what I have by my own struggles", as long as one then says, "my struggles got me nowhere and it was the Divine Grace that illuminated me".

A bit confusing perhaps if we have to wait until it flows

Divine Grace Yoga - Mantra Shakti

"down". (Grace that is).
What's the point of doing anything?
And how come some can get it another does not?

Perhaps the problem lies with promoting either human type attributes to a personal Being or a computer type vagueness that mostly equates karma with just outcomes. "As you sow so ye shall reap". It's perhaps a bit of a leap to think about the Divine Grace as belonging in the field of an impersonality, or atheistic type belief, as surely it can't be a robot like evolutionary "energy"? (Created only by the developing or evolving human mind).

Another way around any conundrum exposed, is to understand that we are covered in ignorance due to the presence of Maya, the "illusory" nature of the world. Lost in a recurrence of our dream, we are just in our ignorance, and we just can't see the Truth. (Groundhog Day)?
That ignorance is our normal self, just our usual everyday personality-based ego.

When we choose to surrender the ego, we get the Grace. Easy on paper!

Divine Grace Yoga - Mantra Shakti

The Grace is there, you have just got to get hold of it, or rather not get hold of it, but position yourself where it flows and be in the stream.

This logically leads to doing an activity that makes things happen and allows Grace to flow.
Do some prayers, try a mantra, and learn to meditate.

Next step is getting some discipline! What about those addictions, and who knows, even obsessive behaviors and attitudes! Get a program which is monitored and supported by someone who knows the way and the ropes. Become: "resting in the hands of the counsellor, guru, or sponsor".

What If the ego says: "no I can't do it I'm just a hopeless drunk", "my depression is too deep", "I am unable to escape an unhappy marriage", or I'm just too plain scared, (to change)? Then perhaps it is time to accept the loss of power of the ego and surrender to receive the Divine Grace. Fix your mind on God your Higher Power or Deity.

What about the atheist?
There will be an alternative way then, (even "spiritually"), if you look. Just as if you go vegan

gluten-free or FOD-map diet, you will find something to meet your nutritional needs. (I am a bit facetious about the atheist bit - sorry).

We still remain bound to the law of action, bound to death, (and taxes), but karma is not our master. Choose the Divine Master and keep trying because when you kind of give up, (selfish seeking), that's when your ego gets weaker.

Well, what about my marriage, children, and career? Desire for a new car, kitchen, or overseas travel? Well do you like the bondage-based years, and years of life and death. Is this freedom for you?
If so carry on!
If not, there may not be another way. (Other than Divine Grace).

Vedanta says *Aham Brahma Asmi.* I am the Divine or Cosmic Consciousness and the world is Maya. (Illusory). This can be seen as religion without a God, and has similarities to Buddhism, which evolved in India post Upanishads. (The scriptures defining Vedanta, which were written at a later stage of the Vedas. (Veda and anta=Vedanta).

Yet conversely, (compared to Vedanta), the other core component of my spiritual practice has been the worship of the Goddess as my personal Deity, which in practice has entailed engaging in Kundalini Yoga. This for me is working with the centers of the body, the chakras, through which the Kundalini passes as it arises from the base of the spine.

This practice is also about Shakti, the Divine Goddess energy, which can be invoked using mantras, especially seed mantras.

So, in some respects this combines both a personal deity with an impersonal deity and some "scientific" practice of working with bodily centers, using the Yogas of meditation, mantra and yoga postures.

This process of being the Divine, as Consciousness itself, may seem contradictory with having a personal deity, but has been in common practice from ancient times as per the writing of the sages and seers in India.

To add to complexity, it is also a surrendering process. That is to leave it up to the God/Goddess or rather give it over to the Goddess. Life events can be seen as an action directed by a force, based on which choice is made by the individual. Such choices, and then endeavors, range from choosing a totally materialistic or even animalistic lifestyle, to choosing a spiritual one, with all manner of variation in between.

The True Self within is so near and yet so hard to find. All the yogis and gurus, they must recommend you ask the question:

Who am I?

We are led to *Practical Enlightenment or Realistic Realization* eventually, as long as we are "on the pathway". We are all full of subconscious material relating to needs and desires but need to experience life through the physical persona in order to transcend the ego. Of course, free will and choice is involved, and I had to make a choice to surrender to the Higher Power, even if it was born of desperation.

Fear of death, of suffering or of life itself, and fear of God.
Of ourselves as potentially Divine.

To have enlightenment, the dark side must be something understood, and life as it is in its grossness, transcended or transmuted. This is *Alchemy*, as at one and the same time being able to transcend and enjoy the true spiritual meaning of *anything* that lies here and now and beyond. Thus, the chaos makes sense.

Thus, the pandemics make sense. Thus, even all the wars of history make sense!

This is also about encountering your true self, which seems covered in fear and suffering. The human ego is in a position to overcome. Transferred beyond, though, or under. Here lies surrender and acceptance, which generates Grace through spiritual practice and selfless actions.

The other prospect is that we get or use what we like and want, and then become addicted to substances or behaviors, which then of course lose their power to pleasure.
So perhaps it will be better for all of us, if we just stay out of the roads. Living in caves and just pass the time. That way we stay out of trouble!

Instead expose yourself to the Divine Grace through your spiritual practice again and again until there is no more "again". And then what life is still goes on. There is still the mortgage, to pay the pets to feed. Then what is just left is the suffering of the moment, the being in the body here now, which is not really a comfortable place by any measure. Life is pretty dangerous, and it can be extremely dangerous. A matter of just survival for so many billions of people.

So, this daily practice is what gives us moment-to-moment relief, (from our suffering), and this is where we can thrive instead of survive.

After some time, we will hopefully have formed a connection with our Deity, with our spiritual pathway, and understand the place of our particular religious beliefs in the whole picture. By this time, we should not be saying there is anything to fix nor anything to make different!

We should be now in the moment, being present, and if we are not really feeling it we should be using all the spiritual practice tools at our disposal. Then there is no excuse, only self-responsibility. There is only the requirement to do what is needed moment to moment and "get on with it". Deal with it, function and provide solutions, as far as one can. Beyond that we are at the mercy of our God!

More likely we are choosing to accept the Truth but only allow it to have overarching dominion only to the degree that we let it be so.
And this is not surrender!

Divine Grace Yoga - Mantra Shakti

Of course we fear letting go, and it is this fear that actually prevents us from letting go. It seems that the fear is based on this: "oh dear I will have nothing left and I will cease to exist".

However, it's true that some personality will remain, even if you become the new Buddha or a big Guru. Also, humans by nature have a flight or fight automatic response, which means that some degree of fear and reactivity also remain. It's all in our nature to be fearful, anxious, and reactive. The spiritual pathway or journey is more than about being in recovery, even though that person seeks "healing" from the past.

Of course, we all want perfect cures, with perfect release from what ails us. Therefore, the therapeutic or self-help managed interventions will have limitations, which is not to say they won't work very well, especially in terms of recovery or remission. The true spiritual path goes, however, into the transcendental and seems to see recovery and remission as almost incidental.

This is when we move into a new way of living in a new home for our soul and enter into the Higher Rooms of existence.
This is when we bring the Divine Light into our

darkness, or we walk into the light and therefore leave the darkness behind. Then perhaps, probably, we hope, we leave behind our negative personalities, or rather all the unhelpful mechanisms in our lives, keeping what's essential for physical well-being. This includes keeping those ingrained petty habits that run their own show. (As long as they do no harm).

Chapter 4

My Indian Journey

·

I spent a period of my ten years in India – 1966 to 1976

    My Journey in *Om Divine Grace Yoga, or Mantra Shakti Yoga* is spread over 58 years. Previous chapters to this contain the introduction, overview and contents of this yogic pathway. Then it is about my personal spiritual journey, which is not a broad autobiography. I have written about my spiritual journey as part of the content in different places my previous books. Now the revision and distillation of that material, with commentary and guidance, is designed to enable practical use by a spiritual practitioner interested in *Om Divine Grace Yoga.* Of course, anything here can be approached as just reading matter of interest.

A lot of my guidance came from the Inner Guru, which can be accessed to get "initiation" and awakening. This component is an important part of my *Om Divine Grace*

Divine Grace Yoga - Mantra Shakti

Yoga experience and can be understood with the explanation of how it worked for me. If inner Divine Guidance is received, there will be appropriate clarity. (This guidance can also be accessed via surrender to one's chosen Sat Guru or Deity). Good intent and practice is required for good results.

Finding a guru.

In 1965 I left England and I spent a year travelling overland until I reached India. I only planned to go as far as Istanbul. However, I found myself on what became known as the "hippy trail".

I was 17 when I left home and 18 when I reached India. I found myself in a spiritual centre called an *ashram*. I met my first *Guru*, (my spiritual teacher) – a *Swami* & *sannyasin* renunciate in ochre robes. I never had at that time any intention of becoming a monk for the next 10 years. My time on route to India and my ten years there are chronicled in *English-Man, Beggar-Man, Holy-Man*.

When I first started to meditate, I found the whole experience very painful, mainly on account of the difficulty I felt sitting cross legged for any length of time. After sitting still for about five minutes my legs would begin firstly to ache mildly and then to send out signals of great pain. I felt that I had to sit as still as a rock to meditate, and I found my lack of body flexibility very frustrating. I practiced yoga asanas (postures) twice daily and began to achieve a degree of suppleness in my limbs.

It took me a few months before I could sit for half an hour in reasonable comfort, but much longer to achieve the lotus posture for even a short time. The lotus posture or *padmasana* is the recommended pose for all serious yogis as it makes possible an upright and straight spinal rigidity, which in turn helps the mind to be freed from bodily distractions. It took me about a year to achieve a comfortable padmasana, and several years before I could sit still for three hours at a stretch.

In meditation when I managed to overcome sleepiness and thoughts about food, I often slipped into dreamy states and visualized all sorts of things totally unconnected with my newfound spiritual life. I imagined scenes in which cowboys and Red Indians fought battles similar to ones I had seen in films as a boy. I visualized pubs, musical groups, family scenes and events from the past, often with great vividness and appropriate colors. From talking to Swamiji and reading yoga treatises I learnt that this mental activity was quite normal for the beginner, and was a cleansing phenomenon, because the memory facilities were being stimulated, by meditation. When a lot of the mind's subconscious material had been "released", then I found that I could meditate without thoughts and visions from this inner level, unless I chose to focus on something in particular.

I was initiated into two mantras by Swamiji. Mantras are words which have a sacred and spiritual significance. I was told that the quickest way to self-realization and mental stillness was by repeating the mantras as frequently as possible until they became automatic. The repetition, or Japa, would concentrate the mind, diverting it inwards from the outer world. When the mind became free from all thought patterns and only the mantra Japa remained, then awareness of the inner peace and bliss would surface, as it were, and replace the different mental moods with an all-enveloping calmness.

Divine Grace Yoga - Mantra Shakti

Anxious to achieve results as quickly as I could, I began to repeat my sacred words over and over endlessly throughout the day. For the purposes of this Japa, I was given some malas, or rosaries of *Tulsi* wood made from the sacred Indian basil plant. For wearing around my neck, I received some knobby beads from the *Rudraksha* tree that grows in Nepal. Rudraksha means the "protection of Rudra" (Shiva). Almost all malas are made of 108 beads. This is the prescribed holy number pertaining to the 108 rishis (sages) who are represented as 108 stars. I was given one later made of 1008 Tulsi beads, a number again having religious significance.

Equipped with all the accoutrements of a serious *Sadhaka*, or practitioner on the Hindu path, I began over the next few months to enter into a regular program of serious meditation, Japa, yoga, and study. I spent any spare time helping in the gardens or in the three ashram temples. A few hours a day were also allocated to listening to Swamiji's lectures and discourses in Satsang. (Association-*sang*, with the wise-*sat)*.

Along with my meditation, Japa and studies, (mainly in Vedanta and the Upanishads), I was learning temple lore and gaining insight into the path of bhakti. I learnt how to clean and prepare the temples and how to offer flowers, incense and other materials whilst uttering the correct Sanskrit incantations. I began to learn hymns and excerpts from the "bible" of Hinduism – the *Bhagavat Gita,* in relatively simple Sanskrit, (once I had learned to read the *Devanagari* script). The interest in the spiritual language of Hinduism gave me, without studying any grammar, an ever-widening vocabulary of both Sanskrit and Hindi words. Within a year I was able to perform the complete temple service for the three small temples and began to do so on my own, to the astonishment of the local devotees who came to worship.

In my studies of the Hindu culture, I became intrigued by the complexities and diversities of its past and present growth. To me, the most baffling aspect was, and still is, the combination of Vedic ritual, image or deity worship and the *Advaita Vedanta,* (pure Monism), and Yoga philosophies. All these major aspects contradict each other in many ways, sometimes going in totally opposite directions.

Divine Grace Yoga - Mantra Shakti

The *Upanishads* expound a philosophy at opposite poles to that of ritualism, sacrifice, and prayers for prosperity, and state that no real happiness can be obtained by following *Vedic* injunctions for the promulgation of wealth and material benefits. Vedanta (or the "end" of the Vedas), is thus the system which even is "anti" the Vedic gods. However, devotion to one's guru (and in later works to one's chosen deity), is strongly advocated in Vedanta treatises as a means towards gaining self-realization. It is also accepted however that Advaita or "a singularity of consciousness", is the ultimate philosophy only for those who have purified themselves in the practices of bhakti, yoga or selfless actions.

After several years I became more and more interested in Shakti worship. Shakti is the female aspect of divine power and consciousness. The goddess whose image is most well-known and popular in India is *Durga*, a many armed figure seated on a tiger. Kali is less widely worshipped, except in Bengal. She has a dark-skinned image and is depicted as holding a sword, carrying a severed head and wearing a necklace of skulls. She is seen as a wild, savage goddess of destruction and in Calcutta, her most famous temple is to be found.

Divine Grace Yoga - Mantra Shakti

Other forms of Shakti include *Saraswati* (the goddess of learning or knowledge) and Lakshmi, (the goddess of wealth). The power of Shakti is also recognized as the body dwelling *Kundalini*, the "coiled serpent" power that dwells at the base of the spine, waiting to be awakened by the right mantra or guru. When Kundalini rises in the body, the energy is perceived to travel upwards through various chakra centers, until it arrives at the thousand petal lotus flower in the crown of the head.

With full awakening, the yogi is supposed to drink the nectar of divine bliss from this chakra and be elevated to a superconscious state of total knowledge. I was not to understand the mysteries of Kundalini until my later years in India, although I did try out various mantras used in Shakti worship (Not from Swamiji but from my own studies.

I had been initiated by Swamiji into various mantras associated with *Vishnu* and *Shiva*, but nothing had been taught to me about Shakti. I realized that Swamiji himself performed a lot of Durga puja and this was his favorite deity. However, he would not initiate me into any mantras in this line and told me that the ones I had were sufficient. It was after this that I began to use my own initiative as far as choice of Sadhana and deities were concerned.

I started to study the relevant scriptural treatises (in Hindi and Sanskrit) and chose my own mantras, discarding the ones given to me by Swamiji. I did not tell him of my new interests because at this time, three and a half years after my arrival, I was tending to go my own way in many other respects.

I came to leave Dehra Dun after four years.

Seeking the *Sat Guru*

I continued with my years of pilgrimage wandering around mainly South India. Searching for what or who?

Eventually I spent a peaceful month or so in an ashram, which was known as the *Vaishnavi* shrine. The head of the place was a sannyasin who had been a distinguished lawyer in Madras. He spoke good English and was fairly unorthodox in his attitude to the spiritual life, by Brahmin standards.

Divine Grace Yoga - Mantra Shakti

I discussed my situation with the ashram guru, *Swami Parthasarathy*, who gave me, without any ceremony, a set of orange cloths. Whether I was officially ordained or not, I would always come up against the criticism of followers of differing paths or gurus. What I actually found was that I could move freely between different sects and their temples and ashrams, simply because I was not particularly affiliated with any sect or guru. I got into the habit of belonging temporarily to various groups of devotees and followers without hampering my non-allegiance to any particular cause.

Finding a *Sat Guru*

Since leaving my first guru, I had been searching for the teacher and path that would seem right for me. I wanted to feel that I had arrived on a spiritual plateau where I had full access to the inner guiding light. I had become half aware in terms of self-knowledge, but I felt unable to live my life as effectively as I wished. The next step after some months spent in Gujrat travelling the Narmada River, was to return towards Bombay, which has been renamed Mumbai. This was in order to visit the ashram of *Swami*

Divine Grace Yoga - Mantra Shakti

Muktananda at Ganesh Puri. (Several hours away by bus).

Swami Muktananda had been wandering the length and breadth of India for years, searching for a perfect guru who would guide him to true self-knowledge. Swami Muktananda found Swami Nityananda, and recieved *Shakti-Paat*, where the guru bestows the necessary grace. Shakti-Paat awakens the disciple's Kundalini Shakti; the sleeping "serpent power" coiled at the base of the spine.

I knew that the awakening of Kundalini could be accompanied by various physical effects, resulting in aspirants going into different trance states, or breaking into bouts of spontaneous dance like movements, (like the whirling and twisting of dervishes). I had read that other effects could occur, like the seeing of bright lights or the hearing of inner music. Personally, I was doubtful, not only of Kundalini, but also of Swami Muktananda's professed power to awaken it in all and sundry.

In spite of my cynicism, I too began to experience trance like states during my meditation and bhajan sessions in the ashram. I began to sway about and then

Divine Grace Yoga - Mantra Shakti

get up and dance in an introspective, blissful mood. However, I rarely went to Babaji's lectures, nor did I go for darshan when Babaji was sitting in the courtyard. In fact, I avoided him and tried to get on with doing my own thing, which *was finding the guru within*. I felt that I was getting the full benefit of whatever spiritual energy was floating around the ashram, even though I did very much as I wished with my spare time.

I stayed at the ashram or ten months and only on three occasions went up to Babaji and asked for some advice. The first time was due to finding that various mantras kept popping up in my mind and turning themselves over and over in seemingly automatic repetition. When I approached Babaji about this he said that the inner Shakti contained all mantras, and the awakening of this as Kundalini was causing the up rise and outflow of them all. Siddhas, he said, had knowledge spontaneously of all mantras and their uses. He recommended that if I was in any doubt about any repetition of a mantra, then I should repeat Om Guru Om.

As well as giving me a mantra, Babaji gave me a new name. He had heard that I had been given a nickname named a well know swami some months before. (It was *London Giri*). However, he said he thought the use of

Divine Grace Yoga – Mantra Shakti

London with Giri was not very appropriate and suggested that I have a proper all Indian name. He told me that I should call myself *Ganesh Giri*, after Ganesh Puri, the name of the local village. Ganesh is actually the elephant form god in Hinduism and is worshipped as the "remover of all obstacles". (*Giri* means "mountain"). I was quite happy to use this new name and dropped completely my previous name with its memories.

Eventually I decided to leave Ganesh Puri with; I felt, a higher degree of self-realization and a better approach to spiritual life.
I landed in a village in a long way from any main roads. Kanod was in some respects a backwater, but there were friendly people keen to see that I became established at the little *kutir* or hut that I called home for three years.

Days, weeks, and months rushed by without really registering themselves. I had no need to clock anything or to regard time as having any influence on me. Christmas and birthdays did not exist for me, and only the big Hindu festivities brought some change into my routine. I was not bothered sitting in my deck chair or cross legged on a rug, about what was happening in the world or how my own life was passing by rapidly. I read no newspapers, I had no radio, or even time piece, and I was not interested in village gossip. I was quite content for long periods to let my *Prarabdha* take its course.

Prarabdha is a Sanskrit term frequently seen in Vedanta texts. It means literally "the fruits of previous actions". A sannyasin is not supposed to do any activity (karma), which would create fresh Prarabdha to be experienced in the next or after life. The ultimate, (and proper), state for such a person is to let the fruits or consequences of previous actions, spend themselves naturally with the passage of time. According to Vedanta theory, Moksha or liberation from the cycle of birth and re-birth is obtained in this manner, i.e. when all Prarabdha is exhausted. Prarabdha is thus the passing of time and events that occur quite spontaneously without push or interference. To passively enjoy or suffer ones Prarabdha might seem to be an extremely negative attitude to life in terms of Western ideals and culture. In the West, the more one does or achieves, (especially materially), the more one is honoured or respected. In India the reverse can be true, and the person who renounces worldly striving and accomplishments is often revered by many as a holy sage or guru.

Divine Grace Yoga - Mantra Shakti

I did not become bored because I found even the most silent passage of time to be full of fascination. The day-to-day growth of a flower, or the scampering of a squirrel could hold my attention indefinitely. I did sometimes think that it would be interesting to be back in England, to use libraries, watch television and be entertained in numerous ways.

I developed then a clearly defined philosophic outlook on life, which was not to change with the passage of time. I gained a deep mental satisfaction from my knowledge of Vedanta, and I find to this day that it guides me towards a calmness and equipoise, which alleviate the ups and downs of everyday life. My practice of yoga brought me to a stage where I had, if I wished, a strong degree of control over my life. This sense of control over circumstances was, and is, mellowed by acceptance by the doctrines of karma and Prarabdha, which means some surrender to the inevitability of fate.

I have a belief that life's events are enacted as ordained, which does work for our ultimate benefit. From this point of view the opposites of pain and pleasure, gain and loss, become equally acceptable. I had discovered that Mukti or Moksha is not a trance like state but simply the ability to accept the world as it is, and ourselves as we are. This does not preclude room for change, or personal endeavour, providing, that is, that one is able to be unaffected by success or failure. Also, that any objective or goal is itself not the only end. The journey, the effort, is also a goal. In terms of Self-Realization, what we seek to be or achieve is already within, already available.

The Self within, is so near and yet so hard to appreciate. All the yogis and Gurus that I most respect, recommend the seeker to ask the question, "Who am I?", and also to seek the guru within as well as without. When we ask ourselves, "Who am I?" we are trying to find out what the true nature of the "I" is. Not the mind, not the body, but an unchanging entity that remains constant in our waking, dream and sleep states. An entity, which remains constant through life. It is the True Self within, which is the same "substance" as the Cosmic Self.

The mind's activities are transient and fickle, whilst the light of yogic awareness burns steadily behind the mental screens. Once having reached the transcendental inner light or awareness, we can return to our chosen life and continue on our way bathed in a subtle serenity.

I was never too worried, however, about being on my own in a corner of some fields without recourse to assistance in case of trouble. I had to accept and believe that the world around me was basically my nurturer and not my enemy. This attitude can be of immense benefit, not just in "wild" places, but also in everyday life. After all, the modern world is itself a dense jungle, which harbours its own multitude of deadly perils, as well as being the provider of innumerable benefits.

Leaving India

In a most intriguing way, I began to dream and think of England and. English things regularly. This was the re awakening, of an area of my mind that had seemed extinct. I started to think in English again, rather than in Hindi, in which I was established. I had a peculiar feeling as if a veil had suddenly been lifted, allowing my previous identity to intermingle with my Indian role. I sensed that my life in India was reaching the point of maturity, and that I could achieve no more in my endeavours there.

Divine Grace Yoga - Mantra Shakti

So, as per my book, I arrived at Heathrow, nearly eleven years after leaving England, somewhat bewildered and took a taxi home to my parents' place. Surprisingly the homecoming was not a shock, but quite a subdued affair. I felt almost as if I had been away on a package tour for a couple of weeks!!!

Divine Grace Yoga - Mantra Shakti

Chapter 5

After India

My Spiritual Journey continued after my return from India, and this is my self- developed "philosophy" of Enlightenment.

In 1977 I felt the dormant yogic flame that had been slowly fading, coming back into my awakening awareness. The sleeping mantras began again to revolve in sluggish brain cells. I even took to sitting down to meditate for brief and infrequent periods.

So as 10 years had gone by in India as a monk, then 10 years passed in the West in the material net, with only the occasional "recourse" to anything spiritual. had the opportunity to spend some years travelling in Europe. (Some of this period, plus later years, is in my book, *Om Divine Grace Journey*).

Seems to me it all just happened! (But was Divinely guided). One of my practices since India was to keep

Divine Grace Yoga - Mantra Shakti

devotion to the Goddess, where I turned to *Durga, Kali, Lakshmi, and Saraswati*. All actually forms of the Shakti, that manifests in our bodies as Kundalini and works through the chakras. (This is covered in depth in *Om Divine Grace*). For me what happened and now happens is under the umbrella of *Life and the Universe*, and is Goddess driven. Thus, I claim my writings, and life, are also Goddess inspired.

Just to clarify I write about Enlightenment in terms of what we can all be, and in fact what we all are all in our Truth.

Accepting one's Divinity is part of the journey, and this is not to denigrate religions or philosophies of duality, as I encourage both a non-dual approach and a devotional one. Religion may however want to us to bow down before *their* gods, higher powers, saviors and avatars. (And no others!). I have though found benefit in many religions, and I believe that religion is a resource to be respected.

We probably have heard eulogies given to the scientific benefits of meditation, relaxation, or quiet prayer. Just try to sit down for 5-10 minutes in absolute stillness with calm and reposed mind. It can be like trying to

Divine Grace Yoga - Mantra Shakti

tame a bucking bronco. The mind is a wild animal. Or part of a relatively civilized mammal called *human*.

To reach a state of perfect happiness, peace or self-knowledge, requires more application than just sitting in medication for half an hour twice daily. To get to a state of perfect yoga, one needs to be perfect yogi. Maybe it's ok for one who can sit in a cave for months at a time, living on a very sparse diet and not watching any TV. However, it doesn't really actually matter whether one is in New York, the Himalayas, or the outback. The setting is not too important, although there are optimum environments, diets and guided practices.

Before the Big Bang: *In the beginning there was the Word.*

If you stay with the sacred sounds, you're connected with all the molecules in the universe, and are at that time, enlightened as a realized human within the milieu that is life. Yes, there is suffering, pain, and struggle, but that is life also.

Realization is the acceptance of life as it is, as a Divine Creation at all times and for all purposes. We at all times are part of the Divine Creation, just as a drop of water is the same water as in the sea. This is not a religious perspective: just what could be the norm of all life, including your own.

The Gunas

There is an interesting description in Sanskrit about three qualities or *Gunas* of nature.
If you are into healthy activities, healthy diet, and engaging in spiritual practice, our nature has some "purity". This is *Sattva Guna.* (*Sattva* means "pure").
If we are engaged in the world of pleasure seeking or engaging in life for material benefit, mainly we are *Rajasic* and in *Rajo Guna.*

If we are living in darkness, addictions, suffering deep mental health problems, we are *Tamasic.* Stuck in *Tamo Guna,* in the darkness
Therefore, there are three qualities of nature, three types of food, three types of activities, and so on.
Have a guess which Guna you are sitting in!

In Sattwa Guna meditation is spontaneous and does not necessarily involve sitting in a quiet room.

However, it becomes also natural to enjoy contact with spiritually minded people, who also meditate, or have some devotional philosophy. Although the Realized person doesn't feel the need to journey to anywhere on this plane or even to follow any rules, that spiritual practice usually mandates "living sanity".

Nevertheless, the qualities of nature still exist, until final Eternal Transcendence. If we are in Sattvic mode we cope with life in equipoise In Sattv*ic* mode though, we may not even be seeking self-realization or engaged spiritually, as we maybe are just happy and satisfied enough, if we are lucky to have this personality type. (Or more likely, have great karma)!

When we are in Sattvic mode we are pure, and we like activities with health giving outcomes, both mental and physical. This means also we eat simple healthy food and avoid Rajasic food. (Think coffee here!). Alcohol is Rajasic, but alcoholic drinking is Tamasic, when it becomes destructive. Going down dark roads and you're sick of it all? It means you're in Tamasic mode

From a realized soul's perspective, the Gunas act at all times, but the soul is the witness of those activities. So, from that perspective technically we can be Enlightened, and yet behave in the mode of any of the

Gunas. E.g., "the drunken master", as described in some Tibetan texts. (It's theoretical)!

Rajasic persons like the pleasures of life: good food and wine, with "life in the fast lane" a popular goal. Then consequently we suffer physical problems from the minor, to severe, such as heart problems, money loss, addictions, and depression/anxiety. We are high sometimes and depressed sometimes. We rage and rant, fueled by desire, and aim for own personal gain. The *Tamasic* road though is only dark, and we may be deeply addicted, but now at a painful level. Violent, stupid or destructive, become descriptive words.

Wisdom Now

I could not say that I was for some years after India, *properly Self-Realized*, as I was predominately in the Rajo Guna state. A lot of us plough our way through this world through our respective careers, marriage, relationships, social experiences, hobbies, interests, and especially desires. So, Rajo Guna often predominates.

However now my philosophy is that a native natural state, (for us all), is to be Divine. (Or at least connected). From that perspective it is relevant to talk about being Realized as our true state within Cosmic Consciousness. Or alternatively we can see ourselves as part & parcel of the Divine presence, which just happens to manifest as Maya, including our embodied form. In Truth, we are not the body/mind and therefore are only the *witness* of our human state. It is the ego attachment with which we identify as *Me.* We then do not identify as Divine Consciousness. Technically it is not necessary to attain anything with regard to the soul and the outer world. However, in so-called reality, we seem to all go on "journeys" to attain what we already have! (This is because of the *ego bondage* that prevents Enlightenment, until it is transcended).

The spiritual practice is being on a pathway that leaves behind the old and gets the understanding that the body is just: "compartments and bits and pieces". Separate seemingly from the Cosmic Reality, yet actually not separate.

Where humans have a major strength, it is in announcing ones essential: "Divineness not *divine-mess*"! With this strength it becomes possible to divert from, go around, go through, and go over all the human weaknesses, including addictions, mental health problems, relationship distress, and physical sickness.

Even financial distress. (Or especially financial distress).

This is not a minor undertaking of course.

Turning everything upside down on its head, opens the individual to unlimited potential. The ego still wants to have a sway and say, "no, no". This is my job, this is my partner, this is my car, etc. etc.

We can move above the level of identification and limitation and find the Truth and Reality. We can't abandon reality, but rather need to work through it, with it, and understand it. Such that it is not one's essential self that is in the way, but one's ego-based life.

So, it's not possible then to say that anyone is ultimately bad, or hard to say something is anything as other than a part of that One Unity. Self-centered judgment is usually based on ego preferences! In saying I am not part of the Divine, I will then need constant help, support, and opportunities to get what I can or grab in the struggle to survive. And I may or may not get this from this life - ever!

Maybe initially this view of the all-enveloping Divine is just an idea of the moment, whilst starting on some spiritual path or religious pursuit. These "elevated" ideas, this kind of knowledge and experience don't usually arise of their own. Something happened to trigger this motivation. Then there can be incentive to follow the assistance of a suitable teacher or guru, or other contact that is more than "just human being". Maybe strong feelings of discomfort are initially engendered about such spiritual dimensions as expressed here. It is the nature of the ego to seek safety in what is known.

At some point however life stops being "what you do for yourself", and the Cosmic Will makes things happen, whether we want them or not. We then see the chaos around in present times.

If we don't jump out of the burning house, we will go up in flames. (Unless we put out the fire).

If we don't see the winds of change blowing and except them, we will suffer simply by being dragged into change unwillingly.

Divine Grace Yoga - Mantra Shakti

It is a choice then to take on board the teachings of the ancient sages and seers, find the sacred and our True place in the universe, align with the divine sounds, or engage in spiritual practices innumerable. It's always as per individual choice, even if initially this only an impulse to get a taste of some spiritual teachings and pathways.

Even religious "persuasions" may have a role to play!

As mentioned, a lot of my guidance came from the Inner Guru, which can be accessed to get "initiation" and awakening. This is how it worked for me.

Continuing my spiritual Journey

Over the next ten years and more I visited various groups for a while, explored Bahaism, and started to resume some of my connection to the Anglican Church. A close family friend encouraged me to attend some rather more evangelical Christian events, often in very large very well attended venues, where they had bands and hymns were on screens. Not really my "cup of tea".

Divine Grace Yoga - Mantra Shakti

Over 30 years I developed a habit of occasionally attending a Sunday service at the Auckland Anglican Cathedral, or other venues if overseas, where I receive Holy Communion. I enjoy the ceremonials, the liturgy, and the choir. I see Jesus Christ as a holy guru worthy of my deepest respect. This is not my main spiritual pathway, and I have no concerns about what others think, as I am Multi-Faith, and I do what I want in terms of my own spiritual journey. That is my business, and I have no time whatsoever for any form of fundamentalism, or even religious people trying to tell me that their religion, or belief, is the only way. Equally I accept what others follow or believe in.

Practical Enlightenment & Realistic Realization

Spiritual practices lead me to a space, a *Higher Room*, from where I am able to connect with my strengths and resilience, and any recovery needed. (It's really about recovery from enmeshment in Maya).

We need a new word then which encompasses "perfection", that is spiritual, (and religious if you really need it), but also acknowledges worldly, physical and mental "fullness or advanced well-being." (Not perfection)!

It's a place where there is a sense of confidence, capability, and ability to resolve life issues as far as realistically possible, and to feel fully spiritually developed, (or fully immersed in the spiritual journey).

It's a place where all the issues of *Life and the Universe*, have been re-identified into the Divine Truth for humans in individual form. With the personality intact! Fears are resolved and individuals can sit in their own Divine Space, Higher Power/Room

Technically then what happens is simply the ongoing experiences of life which happen automatically over the course of time, as karma outcomes.

That realistically enlightened individual no longer acts to get, make, achieve, but rather will experience, (the results of past actions). Teaching or service to others may still take place as per one Deity inspired influence

My phrase then is: *Practical Enlightenment.*
Also, I like *Realistic Realization*

Now this is a sense of being, simply experiencing life, (as if the train ran out of fuel but keeps on rolling).

Divine Grace Yoga - Mantra Shakti

It may be that I became spiritual in the first place, because I struggled with life and it seems that the more I struggled and seemed to "fail", the more spiritual I become or rather the more "desperate"! I had issues at times with living life on life's terms & had an inner urge to "run", (going back to running away from home as a teenager). This "desperation", looking back had been with me since the age of 11. My journey then was not only been about being spiritual, but also about attending to the human struggle. (Which is still spiritual)!

Now, being in *Practical Enlightenment (or Realistic Realization)* after more than 40 years since leaving India, is a relief. However, it has taken me many years to find exactly what works for me, and what works for me may not work for someone else. At the time of writing, I provide some very part time professional counselling alongside my spirituality writing and *Mantra Art*. As a professional I know that I can't just recommend what works for me to some of the people I interact with. However, I can pass on, in my writings, the spiritual activities which have given me the spiritual enlightenment outcome.

Divine Grace Yoga - Mantra Shakti

Let go of the past

It seems to be a normal tendency to look back and say, "oh I did that, why did I do that, what a mistake", or even, "how stupid of me".

In the deepest realized place, it is not necessary to have examination of what happened. If you throw out the garbage, the rubbish, it's just going out, and it's not necessary to check every little bit in the rubbish bag.

Consciousness is the underlying substratum of "how it was, how it is, how it will be". Something else, anything else, just does not have any great meaning. Even so we may want to live in what is a bit of a museum and interpret things over and over.

Therefore, to move into the state of realization, is to be in a place which is essentially undefinable and cannot be connected to by words and language. (Even though religions and spiritual teachings try to).

One's own Divinity is already in perfection, and as for what happened and will happen, it's still within that Cosmic Consciousness.

Divine Grace Yoga - Mantra Shakti

We are what we think, and when we start think Divine, we start to move beyond "mere human". We become what we think.

It does not mean that the world does not exist. Some philosophers and spiritual practitioners call the world illusory. (Maya). That may be just another attempt to explain the inexplicable.

When we experience the Truth of existence, the true reality, we comprehend what I call: *Life and the Universe.*

In the universe we can enter into a nameless space in the ether of the cosmos around us. This is also within our hearts when we meditate. The Divine is not just out there, or not just some god sitting in the clouds growing his beard!

Ideas of God again are the product of history, many religions, and many thoughts of philosophers. Some call it the great Buddhist Void, or *Shunya,* and in Post-Vedic times it was Existence, Knowledge, Bliss, or Sat, Chit, Ananda. The great sages, seers, and teachers say that we are in sync with the truth of God in terms of sound, (becoming form), and can go beyond sound also

Divine Grace Yoga - Mantra Shakti

into the soundless etheric space, The *Akasha*. In any moment and time this present is what is available, what can be known, and this is where the mind can expand in mindfulness meditation to become united with the source of all, or one with the Cosmic Self.

It does not matter too much about negative elements of past journeys, as every experience can also be seen as part of the *Divine learning experience*, and be recognized as totally purposeful. (With no experience needing or any judgement to be added on). When we accept who we are in Truth we claim our Divinity. We claim our Oneness with the Higher Power, the Divine Goddess. (Or God, if you insist). When we do this, we can also begin to demonstrate in our practical lives more than just survival. We move past fear, addictions, depression, anxiety, and whatever it is that troubles us as a human. Again, we accept those experiences of pain through mental struggles as part of Divine Learning. *But,* we move beyond them!

If we continue to choose to deny our own Divinity, we are denying the Divine in all. We remain a human who wants God to fix us, or some other "version" to do so. (The Incarnation, the Guru, the Buddha, the Jesus). We want to be fixed *and* stay human, so that we don't have to take on the enormous responsibility incurred when we fully surrender to Truth.

Most religions will not give you permission! (To be Free).

To embody yourself in your true identity is heretic, and certainly you are not given permission, by most of society, to be "allowed" to realize your Divinity throughout your whole physical body. Then it becomes required that you remain in fear. Fear because of separation. Where there are many there is no Unity. When we are one with the Cosmic Being we become fearless. In fearlessness we lose our anxiety, sadness and our obsessions!

My Practical Enlightenment

My own practice had in India led me to a state where I had the opportunity and ability to control not only major elements of my own life, but also that of others if I wished. (Through yogic powers or siddhis). Somewhat strangely to me when I had taken those "powers" from India into the everyday life of marriage, children, & career, I found that my spiritual energy seemed to have faded!

Divine Grace Yoga - Mantra Shakti

Then I developed an understanding of my philosophy. Then realization of *"Aham Brahma Asmi"*, (I am the Cosmic Soul), is a completely different and more powerful awareness. This philosophy could be called enlightenment or realization. However, I found that true Enlightenment occurs only on completion of the spiritual journey with all components of the worldly experience having co-joint influence.

Looking back questions arise regarding my degree of true spiritual attainment in India. I spent 10 years in India as a monk, and thirty plus years of *normal* life with *normal* struggles. Had I attained some part of the state of self-knowledge and achieved Moksha? (Moksha is equivalent to *Nirvana* which is more common term in Buddhism. Moksha means freedom from the cycle of rebirth, or it just means freedom from this trouble human existence). Release into what? I had I found my own "religion" and philosophy, though only now I can say it has lasting and permanent benefit.

On leaving India I had developed a clearly defined Hindu derived Vedanta philosophical look on life which did not change with in the passage of time. This was not about having multiple gods, sitting in temples, but was about a very monotheistic outlook that was or even atheistic tin some aspects.

Here now I have something that is *Truth Unlimited*, which is unaffected or swayed by any or all religious type beliefs. It is about oneself as the Divine and about Maya, the illusory and transient suffering filled nature of *Life and the Universe*. Vedanta though seemingly nihilistic or fatalistic, has given me the means to develop calmness and equipoise, and helped alleviate the ups and downs of life. This then combined with my Theistic approach to surrender to my Deity, the Goddess, is the final perfection.

It's possibly a conundrum, to have a religious devotion and a somewhat atheistic philosophy! This Higher Power of one's deity can however be seen and experiences as an inner process and taken as just a step towards the ultimate undefined consciousness, where no Gods or Goddesses exist. The purpose of the "belief in God then is to facilitate the surrender process where ego identification is transcended.

I have regained a sense of control over circumstance, which is influenced and self-regulated by my understanding of the workings of Karma and Prarabda, which I have described previously. This means a complex awareness of both the inevitability of some events and the endless possibility for change. Ultimately total self-responsibility leads away from the known spiritual pathways and into the depths of Divine Grace, attained through *Surrender.*

I had a feeling of being powerless over my human condition which seemed to prevail for quite a few years after "settling down" in N.Z. Although this was for a seemingly lengthy period, I believe it gave me eventually a better understanding with better ability to be realized at all levels of the mind/body, *whilst fully in the world.*

Surrender

This seems also like acceptance, where we accept life "as it is" Then, we sit in our awareness and whatever happens is Prarabdha. (The Sanskrit word for the accumulated force of past karma). This is where a *Brahma Gyani* sits. (Knows themselves, as one with the Cosmic Soul, the *Brahman*). Hence the word *Gyana,* which is knowledge of the *Brahman,* the Cosmic Soul. (The individual soul is called the *Atman*).

Divine Grace Yoga - Mantra Shakti

When you surrender spiritually, you stop making or seeking solutions to the uncontrollable. In the 12-step model its: "my life became uncontrollable". (Hence then the need to surrender to a Higher Power). To stop seeking solutions also seems to be about acceptance. Surrender is willful acceptance and yielding to a dominating force and its will. (Which can be your own internal consciousness). Acceptance helps you accept the good and bad equally. So, surrender is also to become aware of the Divine as oneself, with the Higher Power's energy *within*, and to accept it. It involves a shift in belief or approach to the spiritual journey, and is about "Who am I?"

This is a catalyst for enlightenment.

The trust and faith that there is a Divine Force seems to be a pre-requisite for surrender. "I believe that God will help me through this". This requires some awareness generated by questioning that goes on until a belief in the Divine co-exists with access to a spiritual guide. The act of surrender requires some practical substance also. Mediation, prayer, chanting, using a mantra etc. What is the single most powerful tool you use on your spiritual journey? You can't think "I don't have to do anything else", and not do the practice required.

Divine Grace Yoga - Mantra Shakti

By turning your awareness away from normal activity and settling the mind, you can reconnect with your inner space. In the silent spaces beyond thoughts, you surrender to a Sound, the Cosmic Sound. Just as there is noise in life, there is noise in realization. It is very different though and can't be explained, only experienced.

You submerge your ego, which remains, but is transformed into identity as the Divine, where there is the bliss of Oneness. (When you can hear then the Cosmic Sound).

If all else fails, just pray for surrender. It doesn't probably matter who or what you pray to, it matters only that you are willing. The intention to surrender will allow its own release. Who knows, maybe there is an old man up there sitting in the clouds! (For me it's the Goddess, but I'm not saying my beliefs are any less "naïve")! Anything that helps with letting go of fear and unending desire is worth a try.

Again, the small self, the individual "me," is not capable of dropping its own sense of ego, even though the *Atman* is intertwined with the *Brahman*. (Just as water is water, whether in a drop or in a sea). Maybe the "rock bottom" of the addict or a state of impasse, or "the darkest night", triggers some transcendence. A realization "I simply cannot do it, can't win, can't complete, can't change the situation". It is a pity that it may have to occur this way!

Something has to change, even if it is occurring within a state of mental disorder. Someone will come to attend to you even if temporarily, involuntary, as when mental health becomes life threatening.

If, however, you trust the Divine then the Divine Grace leads from darkness to light.

When we agree to participate in the process of surrender to our Higher Power or place our lives in the hands of God then we are met by the Divine Force. The change occurs when there is willingness to access and seek the Truth. This makes us available to be witnessed and to witness. We can then stop hiding and leave the past shames and fears behind. The Divine Self as the individual soul can then be healed by Divine Grace.

Divine Grace Yoga - Mantra Shakti

The issue finally is about being at another level. This is not just about praying to seek the god, the higher power, or one's deity. It's about being in one's own Higher Power, being in the Divine Self, and experiencing Divinity in human bodily form.

Not just: What is this all about?
But also: What do I do (as service)?

Service to others is the life to be lived at this point!

Chapter 6
Post – Enlightenment.

Now my awareness is that there is no religion, or even spiritual belief that I have to defend. I also do not have to follow any path, but I am simply aware of my own choices in this matter. I have opened up to any religious or spiritual experience that helps and accept the need for the many forms that religion and spirituality take. This then has led me to where I am now, in talking about Shakti & *Devi*, (Goddess as opposed to *Deva* - God).

I bypass all spiritual practice hype & confusion, by a surrendering process. That is to leave it up to the Goddess or rather give it over to the Goddess. This can be replicated of course in whatever one's pathway or religion is, and as I am multi-faith I have absolutely no issue whatsoever with doing the same process through any religion or any spiritual practice. I don't have any issue or energy to discuss the benefits of one way or another, and I am simply not interested in debating my religion/s, (or politics). It is irrelevant - get on with the job and attain Enlightenment and Realization!

I discovered that we all walk towards our Nirvana, and simply our world of experience is set up to provide the necessary learnings. (Who made this so)? We can sit back when we see life "as it is and ourselves as we are". This does not cure or even deny room for change or personal growth. Just that one is able to work, without being affected dramatically by success or failure. Also, that any objective is already present as the perfect Self. (The *Atman as one with Brahman*). The journey, the effort is also the goal. Do you live in terms of being self-realized, when what we want is already achieved, and anything else is also certainly achievable? Then one's way of living automatically changes to one of living in the light, and one gets out of the darkness.

I became interested about six years ago in the channeled teachings of the Guides. (See books by Paul Selig where he channels the teachings). Firstly, the goal as expressed is to be free of fear, totally unconditionally, as when one is in the light the darkness doesn't exist. As I did struggle at times with life's fears & anxieties, this had been my goal. If I am honest, when I was a monk in India for those ten years, I was probably still enmeshed in more core human fear

Divine Grace Yoga - Mantra Shakti

of "life & death". Thus, I agree to make the free choice of surrender to the purpose of living in these *Higher Rooms*, and unconditional acceptance of my birthright to be a Divine being. (Under all circumstances). This ties neatly in with my surrender to Goddess Shakti as the world made manifest, & to me acceptance of personal Divinity, via the Vedanta teachings.

This combines both a personal deity with an impersonal deity, and some "scientific" practice of working with bodily centers using the yoga's of meditation, mantra and yoga postures. As well as a focus on chakra energies to connect my mental & physical body to the Goddess Shakti. This may seem contradictory but has been in practice from ancient times as per the writing of the sages and seers in India. They espoused lofty philosophies but also worshiped their chosen or *Ishta* Deity. (Devi, Rama, Shiva etc).

For some time, The Guides gave me some clarity regarding the Gnostic part of my practice. Previously I had human gurus that guided my practice as a monk and into later years. Still a core component of my spiritual practice has been the worship of the Goddess as my personal Deity, which in practice has entailed engaging in Kundalini Yoga. This for me is working with the centers of the body, the chakras, through which the Kundalini passes as it arises from the base of the spine. This practice is also about Shakti, the Divine Goddess energy, which can be invoked using mantas, especially "seed" mantras. A devotion to the Goddess then, alongside my monotheistic or non-dualist philosophic practice. The mantras though are the key activity, and these refer to specific goddess forms, (of the one Divine Shakti). As they are directed to specific chakras in the body, this repetition of mantras purifies to bring light to the human realm. They also work subtly on mental health issues, addictions and obsessions.

The work of the Divine Goddess is about spinning us into the web of Maya, seemingly on the surface. Then to trip us into mundane activities, but really to eventually liberate, as the Divine works happen in the world, and not in some cave or monastery.

As long as we are "on the pathway". We are all full of subconscious material relating to needs and desires but need to experience life through the physical persona in order to transcend the ego. Of course, free will and choice is involved, and I had to make a choice to surrender to this version of Higher Power, even if it was born of desperation. The mantras that I repeat as part of my spiritual way led my individual self into an awareness of Universal Self, expressed as the Cosmic Sound. Eventually this sound can be experienced beyond meditation and bought right down through the chakras of the body to the toes and into all aspects of my life, "out there". *Life and the Universe.*

We are led to:
Practical Enlightenment or Realistic Realization.
Eventually.

Goddess Power

The Goddess represents both Maya in the whole world of human suffering, searching and pleasure seeking, and also represents the link back to the Universal Being, which is formless, pervasive Cosmic Consciousness. (Some people call it God). The Goddess is the energy or Shakti represented by the Kundalini force, which rises up the spine with the human awakening, to break through at the crown of the head, so as to allow the liberation of the soul.

The Goddess is also the focus of the Tantric way that includes the world in worship. Instead of exclusion, there is inclusion of "money, food and sex". (Which is in need often of being dealt with appropriately). The Goddess is the link or a means of transferring human identity to Divine identity by generating the understanding of what my gurus and guides are talking about.

There must be something, some way of living that makes sense in our world, such as that our spiritual being is our essence, & leads us to something super-special. Religion may have some answers and historically has done the job quite well for a lot of people. (And badly for others).

However perhaps modern life views of religion are result of finding out the truth of religious organizations & decrees. This has added up to finding out that you have a Picasso, but it's fake! People may have also enjoyed their faith but discovered it's like black and white TV, (which we had in the 50's). Then we discover there is color TV!

Religion now does not seem to provide the answers to a lot of people in the Western world. In the Eastern worlds, religion is still a foundation of a culturally based society. That also is changing quite rapidly now we have instant worldwide Google, Facebook, and YouTube. As we know, just being in the world, even if our culture is still solid, does not automatically resolve some fundamental doubts & questions.

Becoming free

My years long ago in isolated huts and villages, gave me time and space to consolidate a core foundation Awareness. However, I came to realize one part only of my spiritual journey, which was of a reclusive isolative nature. That I was 50% complete or 50% incomplete! It did take me another forty years to resolve the rest.

The underlying and sometimes automatic subconscious thread of devotion to God still worked for me to enable a Grace that made practical the therapy, recovery, mental wellness, and strength or fortitude. The Western world and my ordinary existence of family, work, and finances has enabled me to understand how the esoteric Eastern based philosophy of Shakti provides true understanding or spirituality. It's at all levels, through all cultures, and also props up the formless non-dual concepts of Vedanta enabling it to be, not just for monks, as traditionally it had been.

Divine Grace Yoga - Mantra Shakti

I am now in the moment, being present. If we are not really feeling this, we should be using all the spiritual practice tools at our disposal. Prayer, mantra, meditation, or other means. Then there is no excuse, only self-responsibility. There is only the requirement to do what is needed moment to moment and "get on with it". Deal with it, function and provide solutions, as far as one can. Beyond that we are at the mercy of our God!

The Guides say we are all Divine, and we all live in a Divine world that is undifferentiated in the sense that this perspective/belief is for everybody. All people have equal opportunity as they are all by birthright Divine beings, in their bodies and human lives. This for me seems a bit more accessible in some ways than Vedanta, which originally was the domain of sannyasins and swamis in India. It is still often seen as being a philosophy in the domain of renunciation and monastic leanings.

Vedanta says *Aham Brahma Asmi*. I am the Divine or Cosmic Consciousness and the world is Maya. (Illusory). This can be seen as religion without a God, and has similarities to Buddhism, which evolved in

India post *Upanishads*. (The scriptures defining Vedanta, which were written at a later stage of the *Vedas*. (*Veda* plus *anta* = Vedanta). The Guides words then come across very much like my philosophy of the Vedanta but placed into much more modern terminology and perspective. The goal the Guides propose is to stay or live in the Higher Rooms where one lives as one's higher self, which then allows all the answers to life questions to flow spontaneously.

The Guides words make it very clear that this "I am Divine', is for the present times for all. This is what we need now in what is a chaotic world of darkness.

I have seen the divine Shakti in visions but have also felt the presence for a long time of a male Divinity that has guided me and supported me. I still identify with the core elements of my "monk person" that I had held for so many years in India. Then I started to feel the female guide spirit, and now there is a combination. (Of the male and female).

I have also sought the guru within as well as without. The Vedanta teachers say that when we ask ourselves, *who am I*, we are trying to find out what the true nature of the "I" is. Not mind, not body, but an unchanging entity, that remains constant through childhood to old age. It is the self within the Atman which is the same substance as the Cosmic Soul. All the teachers of this way point out not only the importance of the guru, but also of the Deity that one surrenders to. The guru within will also be a guide who directs towards the highest energies. This force is also the Higher Power voice.

With my attraction to the Divine comes a natural tendency to serve others, & that is for me a keystone of Christianity. It is in place, even if I have been a bit driven at times by some excessive, obsessive, or pleasure-seeking type common human behaviors. (Just a smidgen)! I can see the goodness in the mistakes I made, but now I can say it's no longer about mistakes, as they are just enriching experiences. I prefer to call them learning experiences. As long as I can still serve others then I am still on the right path!

Though quite different from Christian views, is see the marble form of the "idol" in the temple is a means to help with spiritual practice. It is not worship of a piece of marble, rather a useful means of purifying a psycho emotional mental deficit, and an activity done with a view to developing concentration and awareness. The purpose of any external devotion is that the true nature of one's Divine Self becomes self-evident into all levels of one's human form and existence.

Although I feel and talk of the Divine Spirit including religious reference, it is also useful to place it in view of life experiences in terms of mental wellness, addictive behaviors, and pleasure-seeking lifestyles. (All the baggage that goes with normal human behaviors out there in *Life and the Universe*). The real need is to remain focused on the goal of coming to the Divine awareness, and then find the inner true guru, & to what you know you are in essence.

Your guides: they are you and have purpose as seemingly separate, only to take you to awareness of the Truth, which coincides with the loss of the lower self through transcendence of your ego tendencies. Then you don't need gurus, you are the Guru!

    This is the wakening to the day of the light. Whatever religion or spiritual pathway has got me so far. The purifying benefits in terms of ego transcendence leads to dimming or disappearance of the psycho emotional and addictive tendencies that cause so much havoc in so-called civilized society.

Divine Grace Yoga - Mantra Shakti

Because I see the Universal Spirit as manifesting through the power of the Shakti or Goddess creative Maya, I accept that the energy of Shakti has to be brought into real life. I see the need to deal with and understand this energy as essentially a female aspect of Divinity, without negating the other male aspects of energy in the cosmos. I.e. Is the Cosmic Consciousness – male?

Transactions of ego in all matters, (including psychosexual, and romantic), after I left India, required of me to accept any mental distresses experienced. That meant that the type of existence I continued with for many years thereafter, somewhat "diluted' submerged my spiritual journey into a more common mode of survival. I forgot any kudos I had gleaned as an ex-holy-man. I think I had to become a humble-man not a holy-man. So it was all "good" learning after all.

Life events can be seen as an action directed by a force, based on which choice is made by the individual. Such choices, and then endeavors, range from choosing a totally materialistic or even animalistic lifestyle, to choosing a spiritual one, with all manner of variation in between. The concept of destiny does not make me fatalistic, rather more optimistic, cheerful and serene, due to knowing the true role of the outcome of that destiny. Destiny is my self-responsibility, and what happens is a function of the cosmic laws. Because I believe and feel the central Divinity of the Cosmos, I accept the pain as well as the pleasure of life equally and with equanimity, (because all experience is part of that Divinity).

I made my choices and then sat or fell back unable to process: *Life and the Universe*. My life was unmanageable, and that is when the Divine has come down in the form of grace. And this is spirit guidance. It's a surrender thing! I have realized that the mind's activities are transient and fickle, and the light of yogic awareness burns steadily behind the mental screens. We reach the transcendental through the awareness of the light. Through our deepest subconscious, we can return to our chosen life of being one with Divinity flowing down to all levels of our human endeavor.

The True Self within is so near and yet so hard to find. All the yogis and gurus, they must recommend you ask the question:

      Who am I?

Divine Grace Yoga - Mantra Shakti

Paramhansa Ganesh Giri

Paramhansa Ganesh Giri is my name as a swami, or holy-man. This was the name I used in India and that time is written about in my previous books. The *Giri* part of my name means "mountain". This is the place I am sitting wherever the body is and represents my journey. (As in going up the mountain). In this identity I am on the peak and look down on my small ego personality. Even so at times the surroundings seem precarious and steep. Luckily as a Capricorn I am also a mountain goat and thus well equipped for the terrain! Perhaps this was a design from my Deity to me as my birthday gift. I feel safe, but knowing that if I do go back down, I go back into fears, anxieties and depressions. The days of *should and must* seem to be below the clouds which shroud the lower slopes.

I have learnt that I don't need to justify why I would want to be in a certain spiritual space with a certain spiritual identity. That identity is both enmeshed in my reality as an English man called Raymond and as a monk in India. I can identify with the holy man persona, because I'm seeing more and more that we are all Divine as well as human. Why not also have a spiritual name?

I had a long run of fifty plus years in the Western world with an identity mostly as a "European New Zealander", (as per the cultural line in the census forms). Also, after all, Ganesh Giri only got a few years of use! So, this is a claim of independence based on my search for release from all the attachments.

These attachments do not go away except that in the holy man identity they are covered over by the light of Truth, whereas in the Englishman identity the Light is covered over by the attachments. This dual identity seems to me to be a more realistic situation in the long run. This is identity made at a higher level, as something that I am party to by Divine Grace coming down into my "realistic" life, as I rise up to the Higher Rooms through self-surrender. This is a wonderful creation then, where the Cosmic Conscious can then fully manifest in me through the grace of the Divine Goddess.

Historical data leads to historical expectations, but I refrain from probing more than one day at a time. The historical future is the hysterical future! No more prescriptions for life let alone for medication. The new life is not a new consciousness but rather an acceptance of consciousness as it really is. Acceptance of myself as it really should be, as one investing in Truth.

Is this not freedom? As it is about being and not doing, I am released from the need to prove that I am indeed a *Giri*, the mountain man or rather the *Giribaba* as the "old" wise man on the mountain. I don't need to sit there cross-legged in ochre robes because the first part of my given name from my holy man days is *Ganesh*. (Lord of the *Gunas*). Ganesh as a Deity is the "overcomer of all obstacles", and in Hinduism is invoked before other prayer/religious activities, or to be successful in any human undertakings.

Previous writings have talked about *Gunas*, the qualities of nature, and Ganesh for me simply implies control over my human life aspects. As it is the qualities of nature that function in all life at all times, those qualities nevertheless do not impinge on the True Self of consciousness, which is transcendental. Consciousness is the witness of all, and all means *whatever* we are up to.

This could mean technically, theoretically, that it is ok to indulge in less than pure activities. I know though that the ego personality with the defects of character wants to remain wallowing in addiction, depression anxiety and fear, which are engendered by living with the darker qualities for nature. (*Tamasic/Rajasic*).

All the things that bring fun and enjoyment are not necessarily benefiting any of us. Nevertheless, we can't and we don't want to be living a boring colorless life with no fun. Therefore, the spiritual changes occurring must be naturally easy and be what is desired, (if those changes are to stick).

This is why it's easier to wander along the flat rather than to start climbing up a mountain. It's hard work going up the slopes and the further up we get away from civilization the less amenities we find. In India some of the yogis I found on mountains lived a very sparse life. They may have had tea leaves and collected water from springs. But if you want milk in your tea you're out of luck.

    Don't even ask for a cappuccino!

Divine Grace Yoga - Mantra Shakti

Tara Goddess

I do not practice a wide range of spiritual pathways, even though I am multi faith and have had quite strong connections with a variety of religions and spiritual groups.

I have a Deity in the form of the Goddess, and I practice Kundalini Yoga. I repeat mantras which represent the centres of the body, and also represent certain Goddess forms, (which are not separate from the whole Shakti form). I repeat mantras both to engage in the spiritual path, and to deal with the exasperations of everyday life.

They give me something indescribable but help me clearly to thrive. The bottom line is that I need both my prayer to my Goddess and repetition of mantras for my own sanity. The Goddess takes various forms, but it is the same Divinity that is also the Cosmic Consciousness. There is no real separation. Chakras enable the Goddess Shakti, (power), to flow up and down as the Kundalini through each center from the crown of the head to the base of the spine.

Divine Grace Yoga - Mantra Shakti

My original or initial inner spirit guide has been a reflection of me in my monastic type personality. It seemed to sit on my shoulder in a position and presence such that I have some form of "conversation", as and when needed. It seemed a both male and female energy, as a "reflection" of myself. It was less of an intervening force, more being the voice of wise counsel. This is an energy seemingly separate in some way, and it is something I value strongly.

Whether it's real or not, who knows?

For some reason a few years ago this spirit energy took a new direction as a new energy came to me. This new female energy presented a before my brow area and went down to sit on the right side of my heart. This is still the Goddess energy.

I meditated to find out what name this energy had, and it came to me as *Tam,* the seed name for *Tara Goddess.*

As well as my described previous devotional practice, because of my engagement in Buddhist type meditation with a group, I am aware of the Buddhist Goddesses including *Tara,* the mother Goddess of all the Buddha's. I did not previously know that her sound representation is *Tam*. This sounded to me like a chakra seed "word", as all the chakras have words ssociated with each center. Those words are ascending as: *Lam, Vam, Ram, Yam, Ham, Aum.*

I don't use these words for my Kundalini or chakra meditation, as I use the seed mantas as described in *Om Divine Grace*. (Relating to specific Goddess forms). *Tam* although sounding like another seed sound, is a Divine sound that emanates from the heart of the Goddess Tara.

This is not associated with a chakra center, although the Tara chakra seed sound, (Trim), is pronounced: *Triim*. This sound and form I experience as emanating from my heart area also. (Slightly to the right and slightly outside the body, but attached by "energy cords")

Tara is another form of the Hindu Goddesses with which I am very familiar, but Tara is more popular in Tibetan Buddhism. So, Tara is a Goddess form, which some Tibetan gurus say is also to be visualized as standing level with the eyebrows, or the third eye.

The *Tam* or *Triim* sound is to be visualized emanating from to Goddess, who is seated on a Lotus, and takes a young female form. There are White, Blue and Red Taras.

I am inspired by this Shakti power, whatever form she takes, and hence continue to say, (as in previous books), my writings are Goddess inspired. Now I incorporate the seed mantras of Tara into my daily practice. I put myself into the stream of the Divine Grace through my spiritual practices, but I try not to expect any specific outcomes. This is the outcome of a lifetime!

Fear

There is suffering when there is duality.
Where there is another there is fear.
Life is driven by an underlying fear.
Fear of death, of suffering or of life itself, and fear of God.
This is the pain of life the Buddha talked about: "all life is suffering".
Whatever and wherever the journey or pathway to freedom, one thing is clear. Life is just a sideshow, which is ultimately totally illusory.
Except for pain!

So, it's all Maya! Illusory like a transient dream ending in death.

We need something that works to enable the transcendence of this Maya.

We have to replace it with Truth.

A problem occurs for most of us, because that's not how it works, and that's not how it happens.

If spiritual progress is limited due to limited action, then perhaps only small corners of the darkroom will be lit up. Thus, fear will still be on the agenda. Although it will still have learning purpose. The process is about release, ultimately from all the darkness. Thus, we return in circle to the beginning of the discussion regarding surrender and acceptance.

To worship destruction and darkness in any way seems counterproductive perhaps to the general Western mind. To many in the East, it is very much this God as Destroyer that is sought - to gain safety and security. In the Divine Soul, there is no fear, nor any destruction of anything, because fear is just a human creation. This is the outcome of being engaged in in the human condition, and excepting separation from the encompassing universe, whilst not recognizing Divinity. (Either as one Deity or as the impersonal Cosmic

Consciousness). To accept & move past fear requires the acceptance of destruction and see its true place in the Cosmic Creation.

Pain and suffering make all the theory irrelevant, and can make all our spiritual or religious and therapeutic endeavors almost seem pointless. There is a line of queuing thoughts that like to give fear permission to exist in oneself. However, it's not possible to say fear: "you're out of here". Positive visualizations, however well-meaning, deeming that I am pain-free, just don't work so easily. (They can with continual practice). Know the type of visualization that already has cognition of ourselves as potentially Divine. Then there is some real traction!

Scientists may talk about the function of molecules constantly re-arranging themselves to form things, including humans. Within that concept, see it as a video, film, or play of whatever it is going on, or however you perceive or describe it. It's the process of one's thoughts and understandings about *Life and the Universe*. This includes the thoughts: "I am depressed. I am an addict. "I am a powerful leader", etc. Maybe there should be no problem with just accepting that I am a Divine being really, as why would anyone want all those negative fears, anxieties & doubts? Doesn't make sense! Well possibly it takes time to see it this way and make the necessary corrections.

There needs to be a move past the idea that enlightenment equals: "you are getting what you want, being happy all day and night, and can sort out anything". In Buddhism and Hinduism there are fierce goddesses, depicted in temple icons as cutting off human heads and drinking their blood. Nobody seems to be getting what they want, and yet millions are devotees of the destructive Goddesses, because they do seem to be getting some of what they want. Otherwise, why would they worship that way? There are these forces of destruction that epitomize the nature of this cosmic reality, which in error some religions seek to minimize. "Oh no, our God is not nasty, He's kind and loving". Other religions embrace the Cosmos of Destruction.

Many prefer the more benign & amazing visions, such as of Mary, Mother of God, described as happening in Medjugorje. Or descriptions of someone getting a fantastic vision, being reborn in eureka moments, or having some other transformative experience. To have enlightenment, the dark side must be something understood, and life as it is in its grossness, transcended or transmuted. This is *Alchemy*, being one and at the same time able to transcend and enjoy the true spiritual meaning of anything that lies here and now and beyond. Thus, the chaos makes sense. Thus, the pandemics make sense. Thus, even all the wars of history make sense!

This is also about encountering your true self, which seems covered in fear and suffering. The human ego is in a position to overcome. Go beyond, though, under. Here lies surrender and acceptance, which is generated through spiritual practice and selfless actions. Knowing the true self would lead also to a space where each moment will bring whatever experience we need when they are needed. (Even the fear loaded ones)! Thus, life is lived as also the learning journey, even if yet there is no spiritual clarity. So, if one cannot understand the purpose of pain, dig a little deeper! Then one can understand, pain, death, world chaos, and drill right down to the minutia of personal life.

Divine Grace Yoga - Mantra Shakti

No tigers here!

When I was a child in London I used to dream about tigers a lot, and think they were wandering outside the block of flats that I lived in. I used to read a lot of books about hunting man eating tigers and leopards and lions. After living in India, I came to believe that I'd lived there before, and that all my childhood processes had been regurgitating aspects of a previous life in India. I saw myself as having been a hunter of tigers, who then became a non-violent devotee of tigers. In dreams in India, I saw myself meeting a yogic sage outside a cave and being admonished and turned away from my hunting to become a respectful devotee of the tiger. That dream was about my previous birth: not the current one. I may have been part of the British Raj in India: possibly a collector or some official living upcountry. In India tigers were often a part of my life: certainly spiritually, as the tiger is considered to be the vehicle of the Goddess Durga. However, when I moved away from India, I didn't think then about tigers for quite a few years. My life was not connected like it had been with India and tigers, and my worship of the Goddess. (Now

Divine Grace Yoga - Mantra Shakti

I am very different, and the tiger is a core part of my life).

Finding the Tiger

Interestingly I find that as I relate now to the personality that I left in India as the Hindu monk, I see that my time of ten years in India was probably about sitting in the same space where I am can sit now. (Without the need for a cave!).

Finding the Tiger? The tiger is my soul animal - like a favourite animal but not quite! The tiger represents me as being a complete whole person.

Powerful in that I have my spiritual plane again, but also powerful in that I am a complete human being. I am human with my knowledge of the depths of despair or depression, whilst at the same time have become able to deal with and cope with such elements in my and others lives. This adds to my power just by experience of the common place reality for many. A human life can be, "weak, disabled and dysfunctional". I am happy about this because I don't see it as bad, as within experiences I have also been a functional health professional, a family man, and "healthy human". All

Divine Grace Yoga - Mantra Shakti

this alongside the choice of continuing my practice of spiritual awareness. This is about *Finding the Tiger*: the tiger memories that drove me when I was a child to go to India, and to head off to end up as a monk. This metaphor for life has driven me now to look at the issue of spirituality and religion, and also life's psychological dysfunctions in depth.

Religions talk about redemption and being lifted up. This however occurs when there is surrender, and when there is choice to know one's True Self, accompanied by a willingness to act to make this so.

As I write now in my 70's I can look at my wrinkles, I can experience more tiredness and wonder about all I have done or rather not done. However, the Divine Grace has remained, and I can understand myself as beyond all of this. Certainly, I can understand my identity as the "lord of the qualities of nature who lives as the mountain man". (*Ganesh Giri*). Added to that is not S*wami,* but *Paramhansa.* ("Great Swan").

(Just as the swan floats on water so the Paramhansa floats on the cycle of life & death, (Samsara)*,* without getting "wet". *Samsara* is a Sanskrit word literally meaning "continuous flow", which is the repeating cycle of birth, life, death and rebirth or reincarnation, as seen in Hinduism, Buddhism, Bön and Jainism.

Chapter 7
The Challenge

What's our Purpose?

Who am I? What am I? What is my purpose?
What goes on outside, but taken in through our eyes, thoughts, and are senses?
Thought sees "happenings" as something to hold on to and maintain.
More often we see what we want, but we don't get it.
Why do we do what we do?
Why should it work?
However, if that's what works what's wrong with that?
Then all is well also!
It seems that life has a lot of things that we want or positions we want to attain.
By this time, we should not be saying there is anything to fix nor anything to make different!
Perhaps having a purpose is not all it's made out to be.
Certainly, sometimes it seems there is no purpose at all, to anything.
But other times the sun is shining and all is well.

Another time a person may have deep faith Fundamentalist faith can be akin to burying one's head in the sand.

The other prospect is that we get or use what we like and want, and then become addicted to substances or behaviors, which then of course lose their power to pleasure. So perhaps it will be better for all of us, if we just stay out of off the roads! Living out caves and just pass the time. That way we stay out of trouble!

Presumably there is some underlying understanding that answers must come from within us, in order for us to hold the expectation that some form of salvation occurs this way. Indeed, all the teachers in the spiritual sphere will undoubtedly mention as some component of their teaching that the Divine is within.

My gurus say that the guru is also actually within. So, some say when you find the Buddha tell him to go away, as you don't then need the guru in human form. In other words, you're done, finished you've got it, and you've got what it needs.
Except this is just the beginning!
Step back & look at the real human needs before jumping into space! (Divine space that is).

Divine Grace Yoga - Mantra Shakti

In the spiritual world or in the mental health world, there are other things we can do: activities to participate in. At one level there are talking therapies. We can try to heal through counselling or psychoanalytical methods, or with practical efforts, such as using sensory modulation techniques to alleviate anxiety. Physical relaxation methods: practice controlling the breath, listening to soothing music, or practicing some mindfulness type exercise.

If we go further still, then there are other things we may do. It seems necessary in life to bring in mechanical means to alleviate suffering. An illustration of this is taking medication for physical or mental health problems. We "forcefully" try to resolve the issue. This quite often is reasonably successful, otherwise people would not bother going to doctors or psychiatrists.

We also go into the realm of prayer, using liturgical hymns, or using mantras. Or, on a more physical level, some devotional worship, as for instance performed in temples. We are almost trying to force God to come to the party.

We want to make it happen. Some of it we can touch, talk to, or directly experience through senses, but of course it eventually disappears or vanishes, or changes. Then you need to expose yourself to the Divine Grace through your spiritual practice again and again, until there is no more "again".

And then what life is, still goes on. There is still the mortgage, to pay the pets to feed. Then what is just left is the suffering of the moment, the being in the body here now, which is not really a comfortable place by any measure. The tummy rumbles, the nose itches, it's too hot or too cold, and we are always subject to hunger and thirst, with a need for sleep in a place of safety. Life is pretty dangerous, and it can be extremely dangerous. A matter of just survival for so many billions of people.

So, this daily moment to moment practice is what gives us the moment to moment relief, (from our suffering), and this is where we can thrive instead of survive. By this time, we will have formed a connection with our Deity, with our spiritual pathway, and understand the place of our particular religious beliefs in the whole picture.

Divine Grace Yoga - Mantra Shakti

Enlightenment via a Mantra

Tap into the Divine power within and without. Use and repeat Holy Names. Select the Mantra of choice, or better still get a mantra from a knowledgeable Guru.
Repeat as much as possible.
From India we have for example the mantras:

Hari Om
Soham
Hare Krishna
Rama, Rama.
Om Namah Shivaya

And many, many more.
Also "seed" mantras associated with the chakras-described earlier also.

Mentally repeat the mantra.
Mantra's power will then do the work for you as desired. (I.e. can be used for wealth or spiritual growth. You choose).
Mantra is vibrational healing, of the soul through to mind, body, and to your environment.

Divine Grace Yoga - Mantra Shakti

In addition, mantras create a shield of "armour" around you to protect from curses, violence and accidents. Higher vibration emanating from mantra repetition rises above darkness, or even evil forces.

It is a remedy for depression because you bypass it. It is left behind in the darkness. In the *Higher Rooms* there is only light.

You are not your body and mind. You are the *Witness*. Your natural state is *Sat, Chit, Ananda*. Existence, Knowledge, Bliss.
Light is always you as the Divine soul. It is your birth right. You may need to connect with *It*, even though it is just *there*.

We separate ourselves from Light, we live in darkness.
Change perspective and focus
Seek *Divine Grace*.

The Divine is perfect and complete, and emanations from the Divine, such as this world of *Life and the Universe*, are complete in purpose. Be it your belief in the Goddess as the "*creatrix*", or God as Him, or as the Big Bang. Whatever is produced in this Cosmic Consciousness is interconnected with sound.

Divine Grace Yoga - Mantra Shakti

Even though many components emanate, a wide variety of sounds are associated. A sound for each aspect. (Including chakras). Thus, there are many mantras and each of the major ones has an extensive history of practice and is seated within a body of ancient knowledge.

Our consciousness identifies with matter, the illusion that is Maya. Matter is created and destroyed at some point of time, but nothing really disappears. Hence, we can agree with much of science here. (The Big Bang is after all a "large sound'). However, we are in fear, and rush around, because we cannot understand the essential essence of both the Transcendent Self and the Maya created forms in life. We do not connect with the underlying sound. The mantra makes this connection and gives us understanding to the point of Enlightenment. After all Maya is just the Goddess going about her business!

We do not ask the real questions. Not what is your name, but what sounds are you composed of? Our consciousness is ignored. However, we try to control nature. Unless you know yourself as Divine (in sound), all else is just fleeting experience. A trip!

Divine Grace Yoga - Mantra Shakti

Do not fear, just focus on:
Who am I?
What is reality?
What is experience?
How do I serve?

Find your mantra/s. They will attune you to the collective and the individual consciousness. Sat Chit Ananda.

Mantra is a combination of special sounds and vibrations that purify space, body, mind and consciousness from negative energies. Mantra is an ancient sacred formula that gives a powerful Divine Energy and is the key that opens the way to the Divine Knowledge.

Repeat the mantras as much as possible any number of times.

There is a method regarding repetition. Use a rosary or *mala*.

108 times is considered sacred, as it is the number of Rishis, (or seers), in the sky, as certain star formations. Chant, sing, write, or meditate silently.

The mala is charged with Divine Energy and thus is an excellent talisman or amulet. Treat it with due respect!

Divine Grace Yoga - Mantra Shakti

Get a Guru

The spiritual journey is open to anyone at any time. There are no rules which say you must have a guide, a teacher or a guru. Rather there is an understanding that all focused and energetic efforts on the spiritual journey will bring good rewards. In fact, it is logical that if you have gleaned good solid information, you will get better results, rather than if you accept willy-nilly someone professing guidance, which may lead you into a mess.

Indeed getting "enmeshed" with a guru for the spiritual journey may even be dangerous. So, you need to be prepared for the acceptance of, and then proper use of a teacher, who is "bona fide". Real gurus are not to be trifled with; they are for those who are willing to accept some painful truths. Also, casual acceptance of any teacher may be a gateway for further neurotic anguish rather than peace and bliss. The word guru means "one who leads from darkness to light". A guru must be already in the light to be able to reach out and help others to attain the same illumination. A guru can only affect others to the degree of that guru's own achievement.

Divine Grace Yoga - Mantra Shakti

By taking on a living teacher, one is opening up to immediate evaluation, to being given marks, as in exams, and to being critically examined. The teacher is not working to allow comfort in the student. The student is not working to remain static in knowledge. What benefits then are to be gained by the following of an enlightened being? That teacher, that guru, may not even be alive in a physical sense. As long as the teaching remains with some system or path to be followed, then the aspirant on the spiritual journey can benefit in proportion to the efforts made. The difference with the living human guru is that a dead teacher is not going to come along with a cane to administer a rap on the knuckles. (Which they do in some Zen sects)! What the living guru may require of you personally may be "too much". This may be the very reason why the living guru is necessary. If you want the spiritual journey to proceed apace, you can't stay in your comfort zone!

When the guru is found by a careful, even choosy search, and when the guru is approached in the appropriate manner, then the guru becomes the means for rapid progress on the spiritual journey. It is quite possible to progress spiritually by one's own efforts, and there is nothing inappropriate about this. Using the benefits of an enlightened guide however is like taking the express train rather than the slow goods train that gets "bumped off" into numerous sidings

The Challenge to be Enlightened

To be Transcendental to **all** experience is another matter. This is about going beyond the light and the dark.
Say, you're in darkness. It doesn't matter in this *end - process*.
Until then all you have to do is, strive towards the light, doing the service to others - not hurting others at all.

When you are entitled to participate in the Transcendental event, you move past it all, and you see the unreality, the stupidity and the grossness of human experience. (I am tempted to say all of it, but that may not be very kind!).

If you need to deal with that stuff about being a human, and a sinner or fallen, or whatever - fair enough. However, you don't actually need to, as you are entitled to be a *Realized and Enlightened* being. But it will take a bit of work to get there! (Unless you are already there). Do not listen to what religions and cultural gurus tell you, if they are putting you down, as they want you to stay down on the bottom of the trench. There are reasons for that, and it's all about control.

It's about being a Divine being in a Divine world, which at the same time seems to be a very dysfunctional and disturbed world. This may seem like mission impossible, as it is about being an *avatar* oneself, in the spiritual sense. It also means that possibly you'll be still driving your car, going to work, going to the restaurant, or going to the mall. Think of it as theoretical, if you have to. Just an idea, a bit different from the general view that we are down here and God is up there. This is a view that man has created a God, or is it the other way round? Become separate. No beliefs that. However, one's culture may dictate freedom of religious pathways, and it is not allowable to have divergent views.

We are not going back, only forwards. This is the idea anyway, all time. It's just very few people who accept the inevitability of the future, which will be as designed, or random. It doesn't matter, as the problem is not so much unwillingness to change, but non-acceptance, including of the now moment. We always want something else, something more, better, or less painful, distressful, or boring. So, we leave and come back to the choice of true spiritual growth up to Self – Realisation.

Now, where is the shortcut?
The Truth is, we are in our full Realized status, when we choose to be so. (To start). Is this a hard choice to make? It appears to be a somewhat difficult and unusual choice. Most humans just go about their business, and for many this is mainly about survival.

It may seem to some that we're in an adversarial relationship with God. A view perhaps that God wanted to create his planets and these situations where we're all doomed to a struggle. Then in another almost opposite view, we may accept that there are yogis who can reach out to any other dimension as a perfected Enlightened being.

So, here we are as human beings, feeling stressed in the midst of all of life, and subject to all sorts of uncontrollable events, having limited power most of the time - it seems. However, we are Divine Beings, in the Divine Source, when we look much deeper. Further than our religions "allow us".

Divine Grace Yoga - Mantra Shakti

It's all about the facility of living in Divinity and accessing the perfect well-being that is available to anyone that so chooses. We have been subject to a lot of human philosophy that make no sense currently in our new "internet" worlds. Not nonsense but not working anymore. We are looking here at our level of power that is Enlightenment and Realization, within and without, whatever our circumstance. Then we also do not accept any real division within humanity. We are all equal in this perspective, and this enables us to become more able to work together for the benefit of the whole planet, and hopefully the whole universe.

Is there really a battle between God and humans? We certainly have to fight this illogical experience. Even if we want to fully believe in a male God, and His creation, it's still this unfinished and illogical perspective prevailing. What is the result of this *destruction*? (Let's face it – it's not just *Creation*!). Fight, kill, loot - all the bad stuff, is still going on out there. We are still ready to fight the enemies and win, "with God on our side". This business needs changing, so we can be at peace together, and create something that is functional for all humanity. At all times throughout the world, and throughout the universe. So,

Divine Grace Yoga - Mantra Shakti

are you ready to challenge current views about the laws of the universe and evolution, God's creation, and anything else that no longer makes much as much sense as it did? Give up stuff: which just stuffs you up!

If you are ready, then we are the true revolutionaries as far as *Life and the Universe* goes. There has been a limit to any revolution to date. Nor being one that decides we will make the ultimate changes required for a decent planet. That we may have a perfect experience in life that's worth living.

We need to be aware of our option to be Divine Beings living in a Divine Universe. This may be all it is about, and the rest is "whatever". Are you ready to take this step? Are you ready to be on this journey to the stage of Enlightenment within the human realm? What you do today and now matters. Just being in your Awareness, with each breath, and being ready to transfer out of the mundane into a spiritual awareness. A place where "god" has limited purpose perhaps. Even "creation" is bypassed. We can design our future here, and we need to start doing this now. Or you can choose - maybe next Monday.

Divine Grace Yoga - Mantra Shakti

Life and the Universe is Maya, but there are other ways of seeing this, by entering the state of *Enlightenment or Realization*. Specifically, when in *Practical Enlightenment or Realistic Realization* it all makes sense, and Maya is no longer just some obstacle on the spiritual pathway.

The Cave or the Cappuccino?

We can't so easily wander off to the forest. Even getting to go and live in a monastery has become complicated. Places of sanctuary to actual just walk into and settle down in, are rare, especially in the Westernized world.

So, this is the time for *You* to find Your Inner Guru, and then additionally Your Transcendental state. Can it be done?

Our birth right is our Divinity, whether we are monks, rock stars or plumbers. We are our own Transcendental Guru. Yes, the body/mind provides painful experiences, or as the Buddha says, "all life is suffering". We agree to participate in this delusory activity until we stop pinching ourselves, and start being who we really are. Then the body/mind of ourselves, and the environment of the whole universe, ceases to rule our lives or even have much significance. We escape from *Life and the Universe*.

We may currently struggle with mental health, addictions, trauma, or relationship disasters. Then we might be impelled to shout out: "I am not Divine". Keep on being sad and suffering then if you want to keep on avoiding the Truth of all life. There is nothing between you and Divinity except this business with the great delusion of all life – *Maya*. One can chose to "wake up" in any circumstance and indeed that is what the Transcendental is.

Mission Impossible! If we are truly Divine, why are we not Realised and Enlightened from birth? Also, the evolutionist say we are descended from monkeys anyway, so what hope do we have? We can of course have a God/ Creator who is really in charge and thus get Salvation from this way of thinking, especially if we then are then engaging in some religious activities. It is still then possible to also accept the Cosmic Consciousness perspective and thus so-called humans are then actually sparks of the Cosmic fire. It's about hedging one's bets! Later you can choose a *Him* God or an impersonal Cosmic Awareness. It's about freedom of spiritual choice.

We may seem to be descended from monkeys at times but remember this is still in the ambit of Maya. The monkey-man and the enlightened-man are still in the same ego bound situation, just different levels of intelligence, or spiritual purity. (If there is such a thing).

Just let go and then sit or exist in our natural state which incidentally happens to be Enlightenment. Resting in ones Divine Consciousness. It's all natural and the process is simple. Simple, but how come it doesn't happen?

Lots of followers of many teachers have sat and soaked up the teaching for many years. Yet they are still on the journey, and still seekers of self-realization. What the barrier, and what's blocking the transformative change to Transcendence? Is it ego, or desire, or enmeshment, or….? Probably some mixture that's unique for each individual, meaning that one size doesn't fit all when it comes to the spiritual pathways.

Divine Grace Yoga - Mantra Shakti

Take this perspective! There is no God or Goddess. There is no universe. There are only creations in the mind, which are creations of humans. Therefore, we cannot be Divine with a capital D because consciousness, which is the same as the Cosmic Consciousness, is just our "true normal state. It's who we are. Therefore, perhaps we are divine with a small D. However, people say: "oh my ice cream is divine", so this won't work. Being who you means you are as one with the Divine and therefore being Divine. Therefore, all with a capital D, because it's so important to have that - otherwise we are just humans with egos and minds. Human being itself though is not a cause for uppercase use.

We don't have any concrete position to stay in as humans, because everything changes. Nothing there that is not subject to the reality that all die, and all else will change out of recognition. So, death and taxes are certain, and it's certain that your $40 million Picasso will be dust eventually. This whole position of *Life and the Universe* is just that.

Here belief, is not required, only some logical application to go deeper and deeper into:

>*Who am I?*
>
>*What is this creation?*

Divine Grace Yoga - Mantra Shakti

What am I experiencing in Truth?

The end of suffering

No problem! I am not the mind/body. I witness what's going on. I can still participate, and humans always do just that. Unless Enlightenment has occurred. Then one will be only a witness of events, but not then a true participant. Participation will still occur, but it's spontaneously generated by the accumulation of past impressions, activities, habits etc. Like a motor that ran out of fuel but keeps rolling on, for a while. The Realized being is aware of, say an itch, and may scratch. This experiencing and continued reaction to itches etc., is Prarabdha, the accumulate effects of past *Karma*. In this case only the qualities of nature, called Gunas, are acting. (Again, still only in the domain of Maya – that illusory nature of what we call real). There is no more bondage, as it's just the residue of *Life and the Universe*, doing its own thing as it was set up to do. It was set up due to desire, which is that wish to participate in life to satisfy our desires and wants. Not necessarily sex 'n drugs 'n rock 'n roll, but having families, careers all the thing that we monkeys have evolved into, and are now participating in. (Evolutionary superior humans that is). A flash car?

Divine Grace Yoga - Mantra Shakti

That wonderful wardrobe of clothes? Easy! What about being rich and famous, or a film/rock star? Famous writer/artist perhaps?

This is where we get bogged down, and our superiority as far as evolution is concerned, is questionable. We stay living in Samsara, taking birth after birth, and experiencing death after death. Until that is, we become disinterested in it all. We are not suicidal then! We are sane! (Nor depressed – just sad about it all). There may be a sense of loss and difficulties with adjustment. That is why when we turn deeply to the spiritual, or even religious life, there is created a possible new set of problems. The ego might fight back and increase the cravings and release a temporary insane splurge into addictive or obsessive behaviour. Depression may seem real. (It isn't – its temporary).

Suffering has no end! But it also has no beginning. If you can get to the situation before the beginning, you disconnect suffering from life. All life. *Life and the Universe.*

How to do this? Start by finding out if you are the "doer". Do you create your life and why? There is no real reason why you need to be in this human form on this planet. No reason!

If then the insistence to remain human continues, only reduction of suffering is possible. Mental health issues for instance can be alleviated if the right approach is made. (That is a huge problem area in itself because of the current overwhelming reliance on medications). So, the end of suffering is a mirage mostly because the core reasons for its existence remain. Thus, whatever gurus and religions and various new age of self-help teachers says: this is actually a no-go area. It is no-man's land because you are not allowed to walk over the border to the "other side" if you want to bring all your baggage. You have to be prepared to discard everything, abandon everything. And, who wants to do that! Ever the most advance spiritual practitioners will want to hold onto their achievements. That could be spiritual centres, writing, and students. Anything that is - "all that is near and dear to me". And then, there are relationships to be placed in their proper place. What does that mean! Well, it is not about abandoning anyone, but it is about cutting negative ties, dependence, obsessions, and really this whole human connection business for self-purpose. But it's not about loss. It's about gain and transformation, especially in regard to relationships.

Divine Grace Yoga - Mantra Shakti

This is where everyone gets stuck and thus stays in Samsara and keeps coming back for multiple re-berths. Yes, heaven can last a while, but if you want to be human again you will find a way back. Some religions don't even know what really goes on after death – they just make up stories about Heaven and Hell! Ignorance does not provide ultimate liberation from the cycle of life and death, just maybe some solace. So, yes "religion is the medication of the masses". (Marx said it is the *opium* or the masses).

Next accept each moment as the only one, the last one, the full experience of all there is or can be. This seems extremely painful. That's because the pain of life is being magnified and concentrated into this one moment. This is when it all can be transcended, but you need to know what you are doing, and be your own guru mostly, for the moment-to-moment awareness. Then you are the Transcendental Guru, because you are willing to accept that the massed negativity of the moment is only the ego, just Maya. Samsara is what you are in, and to transcend it you can't go anywhere. You can't get from non-realised to Realized with this Transcendence, because it's not a journey. It's more of an experiential activity. Be your own Being and become therefore in tune with Cosmic Consciousness - not separate. Therefore, whole and complete. You are then done here! (And don't then need to do anything about it all and start changing everything).

Best not to do anything about confusion and doubts, especially any "rage against the machine". "Why won't god/higher power/my personal god form fix it"? Because you are responsible and there is no god/higher power/personal god who will save you. You can fantasise that this, (being fixed), is the case and "this is what happened personally to me". It won't last! Ultimately Jesus, Buddha or Krishna etc. won't fix it, because it's your job to learn from life and sort it out - all on your own. That is what empowerment is all about. Divine Grace will just give you the ability to get there – not provide the fixing it stuff we all desire so much. When you calm down from your tantrums about life you will be ready for the Big Step.

Now we have a situation regarding *Life and the Universe*, where nearly all humans are entrenched in their identity with race, culture, religion etc. Nothing to comment much on here, except that so far history has been about wars and destruction a lot of the time. So much for culture and religions! Never mind, it is a learning environment that we suffer in – Samsara.

Divine Grace Yoga - Mantra Shakti

Until, that is, we move up a few levels. Move into spiritual practice as well as advanced human practice. Then we think about doing stuff for our Higher Purpose, (or Higher Power). Then, maybe, we advance enough to make service to others our priority. Eventually for the Bodhisattva, the Jesus, and the Krishna, it's only about being the Avatar of Divineness on earth, for the sake of humanity. We are then beyond all levels, as this is where we see and feel and realise our essential nature in relation the Cosmos and all its life. First thing first though, and that is about how to move past this human ego-based life of selfishness, and how to have some sense of spiritual sanity? We already know that we are responsible for our actions – no gods to the rescue! This is then our moment-to-moment business, otherwise we stay where we are.

The mind doesn't want to be trained or curtailed, so it doesn't seem doable, unless you can sit in a cave with no distractions for months on end. The mind can settle down like sediment falling to the bottom of a still lake. In this busy world – forget about it! So, yoga needs to be more structural, with practices that allow one to separate out from the mind and the world, whilst in the midst of it. I use mantras. That's it for me. That's all I do, per breath, per moment. No matter what I do, right

Divine Grace Yoga - Mantra Shakti

or wrong, or what happened, or what's going on now. I take refuge in the mantras that I use, (and there is a selection, just as one wears different clothes for different occasions). It's a refuge and a stable mountain of attention. Ultimately the mantra is transcendent through its own sound connection to the Cosmic Sound.

Truth is the "I" of you as the Divine Soul. It is your birth right. You may need to connect with it, (it seems), even though it is just *there*. You have to sit on your mountain, (of solid spiritual practice), and chant through the time of the dark clouds and the storms.

We separate ourselves from Light, we live in darkness.
Change perspective and focus
Seek Divine Grace. The Light will shine through, and with it the Divine Sound will manifest.

Our consciousness identifies with matter as ego, and the illusion that is *Maya,* gets created, but also can be destroyed eventually. Nothing really disappears, because nothing really appears – illusory stuff all of it. We can agree or disagree with much of science, as per choice, but the Big Bang is after all a "large sound'. It's just mind perspectives still, and not so relevant in the state of Enlightenment, and confused views of science are not the position of the Transcendental One. However, we are in fear, and rush around, because we cannot find ourselves experiencing being the Transcendent One, and truly seeing the unreality of the Maya forms created in life. We do not connect with the underlying sound then. The mantra makes this connection, (somewhat artificially it is true), and tales us to the point of Enlightenment. Then Maya is seen as just the Goddess going about her business!

Attachments

Unfortunately, attachments will remain in the soul memory and affect future passage onwards, even after death. This will be especially so if predominant negative thoughts remain to the time of death. Some type of obsession, addiction or just plain old lust may have a regressive effect regarding next realm entry. Fortunately, the power of mantra and faith will cut through the bonds eventually, even if it seems there is some delay as these things take time. Be patient with the short trial which occurs also while practicing devotional yoga, and mantra repetition, and allow the onward journey to pick up successful in its own time. (Gods will - not my will). Surrender to the Divine Grace and allow to be cleared away what you can't control or overcome.

The last dominant thought is very important, and if we are dependent on our spiritual practice, then we will remember what we need to at death. Even if you think you are such a sinner or bad person, invoke your mantra at the point of death. The emissaries of darkness will be held back. There seems to be some confusion or very different ideas about the time of death as per various religions, and within the "holy books". Take only what you need for sanity! What makes sense and seems productive. The writings of those who are Realized are more important, as they have had the experience and can better advise accordingly.

Chapter 8

Being Divine

I am the Divine – please God help me!

True spirituality then is a radical perspective that accepts the move towards the transcendental, whilst yet being still in human state. It's about being in one's own Divinity yet paradoxically finding that through external spiritual guides or through Divine Grace. This is very strange, because if indeed the guru is within, why is a "guru without" needed? If I am really a Divine presence, (beyond the human), why can't I do it myself? (Getting to self-realization that is). In the pure Vedanta view, we are all, already realized, and it's only a cloak of Maya that is deluding us. You can read about the initiation of this view in the Upanishads written at the end of the Vedic period. There are also many later writings about the philosophies involved, and this continued over the millennia until the present time. The philosophies were set up in ancient India, but in modern times there are some Western self-help writers who lean toward or borrow from Vedanta views.

It is very hard to make the spiritual changes required to be realized and is not easily done under one's own human power. It is a bit like asking a drunk to walk in a straight line. When you are affected by intoxication you cannot just do stuff! In this case you can't go from A to B because you already at B. You just don't know it. Or rather, that is not one's experience, realization, and hence perception regarding the mind-set.

No matter how intellectually spiritually astute one becomes, if you remain in a certain headspace of basically ego focused need, you ultimately go nowhere. This spiritual dimension cannot be made or experienced by the brain's electro chemical processes. Even if science takes us to longevity, even immortality. and cures all mental deficiencies. Researchers cannot be trusted with God! This is why we need external Divine interventions, which technically, or rather, as far as some of the ancient teaching goes, come from our own generated spiritual activities. We need to give up on our ego struggle and let our Deity come to the party. We enter, or rather simply exist in, a place powered by something other than who we thought we were. The deeper we go, the more an easier path it becomes, with less frustration about what's going on in so-called real life.

It can seem like our Deity or God is taking over, once we have come to be within the preserve of the Buddha, or Jesus, or Krishna. It is through a simple natural native Divinity that has been uncovered, and then allowed to be in-charge. By all means stay with the personal external gods, guru, incarnation etc., if that is the choice or status quo. The spiritual experience can be is mostly the same, as what still is the case is that *Sat, Chit, Ananda* or Existence, Knowledge, Bliss. A choice is made to experience this state as a formless position or as one with form. (Having then the presence of one's Deity)

The impossible is the nothing. Everything is on the table. Then the spiritual reaction is per moment-to-moment life practice. This practice is real in this life in some sense, as I am the witness of it like as in a dream. Though, I am truly real as a spiritual being. Experience all within and without, as Divine, when connected to the eternal Divine Consciousness. Oneness is like being just a one is a drop of water, which is not different from all the water in a lake. Eventually that drop of consciousness merges into the Consciousness.

It's all about sex – or is it?

I suppose it comes back down to sex. Even until the end of life the urge to engage in sexual activity can be quite strong. The urge to procreate has been not just strong, but a foundation of life. It's driven is driven by a few chemicals in the body and unfortunately human beings make a huge deal out of it. For many it is the be all and end all of life. Sometimes through old-age or physical conditions the sex drive is significantly reduced. However generally it's not so, and either natural impulse or desire marks the processes involved. Why wouldn't it be so as really we are driven by sex for propagation of our future, plus also recreation interest? It's a major backdrop to all our life experience, activity, and general being.

So why is it such a problem? Why is it such a problem in regard to religion, spirituality, and the lives of nuns or monks, (as an extreme example)? Is it a problem because we have made it so, as we have made it more than it really is in importance? Is it because we have made it into something that we are fascinated, obsessed and addicted to by most in general? I hesitate to say, "in general", but because the statistics are there, it's throughout the population at a quite dysfunctional pervasive level - quite possibly!

Now where do we go with this if we want to have spiritual enlightenment, or deep connection with the Divine, or some release from the cycle of birth and death? Or to even make sure we go to heaven?

If you look at the Hindu gods and goddesses, all the main gods are male, and they all have female consorts in mythology. They also have progeny, or quite often they have something similar to harems or polygamy. So yes, it has been that sexual prowess in those historic terms seemed to be part of the lifestyles of powerful men, including the prophets of religious history. Ignoring this historical patriarchy and scripture injunctions, the issue is whether the sex drive is compatible with the spiritual journey, or if it creates some problems. (It does)!

Does sex create problems for everyone? Even if it doesn't, then the outcome of sexual activity is more progeny, which is surely a problem in terms of the capacity of the earth and numbers of people to feed. Some say this is a major problem. Too many people all generated through sexual activity!

There is another way of seeing things. This is to say that sex is a means and some help in our spiritual journey. This is the view of some who practice Tantric philosophy. Actually, it is the view of Tantra that sex is inseparable from the spiritual journey and more or less necessary for it. In the tantric view you have to have sex with 100% undivided attention, in order to be on track with your meditation!

The truth is probably somewhere in between all views or any extremes, as previously mentioned or hinted at. Sex is driven by chemistry in the body and as a side issue, most of our mental health problems are, (so we are told), Just driven by neurochemical activities. A lot of what we are really concerned about here is actually very simple - just functions as a result of having a body and brain.

Not a big deal then! Well, it's not a big deal if you have means of moving past the limitations, the patriarchy, the mind/body conundrum, the religious injunctions, the societal norms, and especially any hormonal imbalance or excess.

This is promotion for the tantric path of meditating on the kundalini and associated chakras, using mantras is associated with those centres. You want something that will crossover and connect the Divine from the mundane, (including sex activity). Just like connecting strengths/skills to actions. Do you want to connect the natural energy to natural actions leading to natural Realisation?
In the Divine there's no good and bad. Sex is somewhat irrelevant down the track maybe, but it is now extremely relevant and powerful as a tool to enhance higher consciousness attainment.

Recognise the energy of the chakras, particular those lower chakras allied to sexual energies. Find out the mantra associated and incorporate them in one's mental repetitions of mantras. By doing so, there will be generated a connection from the sexual content of the body to the inherent underlying sound of that content, which relates to the subtle energy of the transcendent Divine.

In the Divine the sexual energy is very potent and strong, because it is about unity. It's seen as such in some figurines of the Hindu/Tibetan pantheon. They are in union of sexual congress. There are also images of God/ Goddess is being as one body - half and half. This Divine Union - where is it? It's where the sex drive between two has been united - two to become one. "The two shall become one flesh", which historically has meant a union of man and wife. Nevertheless, the union can be achieved between any two, despite what religious instructions or injunctions say. Simply it is about union that becomes spiritual, because two beings are merged into one. This is also the root origination of this whole business of falling in love, making a connection, finding a life/soul partner.

So don't underestimate sex in the spiritual journey. It is overarching, over powerful, and everywhere, and we need to be with it, use it, and not get into addictions or obsessions, nor crazy relationships because of it. We can place our practice in in tantric activities as a means to greater Divine Union.

Divine Grace Yoga - Mantra Shakti

Mental health & science

Find the True Self – then you are the Transcendental One. Then……?

That there is scientific research about spirituality and mental health is telling. Somehow science has lost the plot and now wants to go back to the Stone Age when human began worshiping. Why are scientists interested in something that millions have accepted for thousands of years? It's even reaching into psychiatry with the neuroscientific exploration of religious and spiritual phenomena. In other words, let's prove that it's all in the mind. So, for once psychiatry has got it spot on. Yes, it is all in the mind! *Life and the Universe*: everything and anything is but a product of Maya, which is if drilled down to individual level, is but a mind product. It's all fantasy, so why treat it? With medication, therapy, etc.? Actually, medication use is very logical. We eat food, we ingest substances, and we have always been a bunch of self-medicators. Goes with the territory, so don't knock those clever chemists who seek to make us feel good. And yes, science will enable us to live forever and beat all diseases and be happy. Yeah right! Whatever. Do you want to stay in Samsara and continue to suffer? Forever? If not, then do not live forever - ever!

The Divine is perfect and complete, and emanations from the Divine, such as this world of *Life and the Universe*, are complete in purpose, though it all seems crazy from a disturbed mind perspective. Be it your belief in the Goddess as the creatrix, or God as Him, or as the Big Bang. Whatever is produced in this Cosmic Consciousness is interconnected with sound. Therefore, the mantra will heal the craziness and allow different perspectives. It can seem very slow, especially if you are feeling some agitation. Remember though, you are not your body and mind. You are the "witness". Your natural state is *Sat, Chit, Ananda.* - Existence, Knowledge, Bliss.

Science may have advanced regarding longevity. This field of research is still in its early stages, so most of us will be "dead and gone" before the wonders of this new "new age" hits us. There will be an ever-increasing interest in doing a science based, advancement of life on earth. (An earth which may not exist due to global warming, wars, Covid etc.). However, the main issue seems to be avoided – what is our True purpose? Then there is the pursuit of scientific evidence for the existence of God. (So, it gets weirder).

At least there is a growing and significant consideration of spirituality even at a scientific level. This may be happening more and more in the world, even though the daily news says we are doomed to kill each other, or some pandemic will do the job.

Now here is my: Get well – scientifically proven advice.

Read the first few chapters on how to engage in Om Divine Grace Yoga.

Attachments & mental health

Unfortunately, attachments will remain in the soul memory and affect future passage onwards, even after death. This will be especially so if predominant negative thoughts remain to the time of death. Some type of obsession, addiction or just plain old lust may have a regressive effect regarding next realm entry. Fortunately, the power of mantra and faith will cut through the bonds eventually, even it seems there is some delay. Be patient with the short trial which occurs also while practicing the devotions, meditation yoga, or mantra repetition, and allow the onward journey to pick up successful in its own time. (Seek also God's, will - not my will). Surrender to the Divine Grace to allow what you can't control or overcome, to be cleared away.

The last dominant thought is very important, and if we are dependent on our spiritual practice, then we will remember what we need to at death. Even if you think you are such a sinner or bad person, invoke your mantra at the point of death. The emissaries of darkness will be held back. There is a lot of confusion involved in all religions within the "holy books" but take only what you need for sanity. What makes sense and seems productive. The writings of those who have been realized are more important, as they have had the experience and can better advise accordingly.

Religion and spirituality issues have become more in recent times, part of a mental health clinician's initial evaluation, or assessment. That doesn't address the issue of human desire and attachment, nor the consequences of that. It's a clinical direction that often defers to culture, political correctness, religious groups etc. without really understanding how all the mental health issues are is bound up with, or concurrent with spirituality. Therapy and counselling services may look at the issues in part, but may not revisit this area during treatment, once any initial assessment phase is over.

Some researchers now point to the association of spiritual values with psychiatric disorders, and make comparisons for instance, to worship frequency. Then there is the issue of, say, a religious or spiritual person who develops mania or a psychosis, with seemingly obsession about their belief to a dangerous point. Remember that whatever is normal for a person, as part of personality expression, may also be expressed as quite disordered religious thinking. Historically, persons with "crazy" thinking or behavior were often seen in a different light by the public and even put on a pedestal! Unfortunately, though they could be seen as possessed or witches with fatal consequences. I have not seen and met or read of any spiritual advanced being, who was not at some stage intimately involved with religion in some form. Why would anyone with mental health disorders not have the same involvement? It's just the mind disorder that "skews" things. (Yes, of course, there are severe clinically diagnosed disorders of the mind which need professional input, due to the danger presented to the individual and others).

Divine Grace Yoga - Mantra Shakti

It's the spiritual journey that addresses the issue of human life *attachments*. This thought could be made without any reference to or involvement with religion, either as belief or practice or as morals. Many say, "I am not religious", without seeing that a lot of their spiritual practices historically were part of organized religions. Religion and spiritual practice may seem to go hand in hand then, although nowadays this relationship seems more tenuous and even hostile at times. The spiritual seeker may find at a certain stage, a burning desire or motivation to escape from or leave behind all or some of previously held religious beliefs and practices. Many gurus also seem to imply that at the higher stage of spiritual practice you move on from religion, and even from the teachers and teachings that you started out with. So, theoretically, the spiritual journey could be made without any reference to, or involvement with, religion, either as belief or practice or as morals. Yet, I have not seen, met, or read of any spiritual advanced being who was not at some stage involved with religion in some form.

The semi-naked yogis in India are *Avadhootas*.

(Meaning "without form"). They are revered as very holy as they give up all attachments, including sometimes social and religious restraints or rules. They can appear to be mentally unwell or to have significant psychiatric issues. These crazy adepts in certain spiritual traditions are practicing as they are, often after being immersed in a religious culture, and then move past the restraints. They still are accepted as being culturally acceptable by the general public in India. They are held in high esteem and are visited sometimes by multitudes of devotees. They sometime go on to build, (around them), quite large ashrams. (Or rather. their followers do this work). They are however "unattached", (one hopes)!

In some other religions today, this renunciation is almost a deviance from the accepted moral and social rule. So, this non-attachment can even be seen as a sin or a moral deviation.

The spiritual journey is about the goal, the end product, notwithstanding the connections made on the way with organized religion, New Age ideas, and evidence-based therapies. Religion etc. becomes a block to spiritual growth when it interferes with, or is allowed to, block further evolution. The concepts of God, deities, messiahs, and avatars or incarnations, belongs to the realm of the practitioner but not to the world of the Realized One, who has become awakened, enlightened or divinely fulfilled. That goal is really quite anarchic, disinhibited, and even destructive in terms of what passes as conventional ways of equating ordinary life with the Higher Power. It might seem to indicate a madness, psychosis even, or perhaps almost catatonic depression, as some yogis have presented. (See my descriptions of such yogis in my book: *English-Man, Beggar-Man, Holy-Man*).

Devotion which derives from or is associated with the East (Hindu, Buddhism and others), is sometimes contrasted in a negative way with the Western scientific civilizations, and traditions of Christian and Jewish monotheism. In regard to some of the New Age practices, they are often contrasted with science or religion and can be in this basket. Some though, have presented alternative therapy modes, which have become more mainstream, and even for instance, more acceptable to conservative Christians. On the positive, there does seem to be an amalgamating or synthesizing impetus happening, which could lead to total holistic approach to the concept of wellbeing and awareness. It comes out even in the current "trendy mindfulness" explosion, and the being "woke" stance. This seems good reason to say there is a revolution potential, for practices that have wide appeal to different people, who then have what seems to be new outlook on spiritual searching endeavors. It probably is actually a synthesis of what has gone before, and not a revolution. People now more often seem to want religion that is non-judgemental and accepts a variety of beliefs. This is worlds away from fundamentalism, which also fights back to maintain its traditional power base.

Appendix

Refresher of the main component topics

What is?

Vedanta: Means literally end of the *Vedas* and is a part of the vastness of Hindu philosophy. Vedanta however, on the surface, seems to oppose the Vedic & Hindu religion in a major way and on major points, and separates away from the concept of worshipping many gods or performing rituals. God is one transcendental state, without specifically denying the value and purpose of a personal god. It does critically analyse Vedic sacrifice and worship of the various deities, and even penance of the yogis.

Vedanta seeks to clear away the clutter of ritual, and point to the discovery of the inner soul, the *Atma*, which is one with the cosmic soul, *Brahma*. Vedanta is not the pathway of devotion to a Personal God. It is a way of being already perfected souls in oneness with the whole of creation. It may be hard to swallow, that we ourselves are God, as the Atma is the same substance as Brahma. The Vedantic mantra is *Tat Twam Asmi* – That I Am. Or the mantra, *Soham* – I am that (Brahma), meditated on with the inhalations and exhalations of breath. I am Brahma, Cosmic Consciousness

Kundalini: Otherwise known as the serpent power, which is considered to be like a coiled snake of energy at the base of the spine. It can be coiled there in a dormant state & when awakened the energy or *Shakti* arises in a sinuous movement through the centre of the spine to the crown of the head. Along the way are centres of energy called *chakras* and each one of those chakras has specific and particular attributes.

Shakti: Considered to be the universal energy or Goddess energy - the creation force of the divine being. In this sense the masculine aspect of divine being is seen as a transcendental power which is beyond form and shape & the female aspect is seen as the external creation. When practitioners worship the Shakti or Goddess form, they can worship the divine being as the world, the universe, or creation.

Mantra: Is a Sanskrit word. The first part of the word means "constant thinking of" The second part of the word means "that by which one is protected."

So, by the conscience thinking of a certain word one is "protected', where the word protection has a wider connotation in spiritual terms, as being a means to a degree of perfection (*siddhi*). The part *Man* means literally to think and the word *Tra* means literally to protect or free. The repetition or use of a mantra is considered to be enabling of a range of outcomes, from enlightenment down to the acquisition of wealth and pleasure.

The repetition of a mantra is called *Japa*. In Hinduism it is said in Scriptures that in this age, the Dark Age, (*Kali Yuga*), that the repetition of certain mantras is the easiest way to obtain enlightenment. However, there may not seem to be much science or evidence associated with such a view.

Chakra: In Sanskrit, chakra translates into "wheel". These "wheels" can be thought of as vortexes that both receive & radiate energy. There are seven major energy centres or chakras, in the human body. They run from the base of the spine to the crown of the head. Emotions, physical health, & mental clarity affect how well each chakra can filter energy. This in turn dictates how pure the energy is that's emitted from different regions of the body.

Divine Grace Yoga - Mantra Shakti

Seed mantras with their chakras - (My core teaching)

Om (Source of all). **Sahasraram Chakra** - Crown chakra

Om (Source of all). *Ajna* **Chakra** 3rd eye - OM

AIM – (pronounce Aiim), Bija mantra of *Saraswati*, ***Vishuddha* Chakra** - Throat chakra

HRIM - (pronounced Hreem), mantra of Divine Maya.. ***Anahata* Chakra** - Heart Chakra.

SHRIM - (pronounced Shreem), relating to *Lakshmi*. ***Manipura* Chakra** - Solar plexus chakra.

KRIM – Krim, (pronounced Kreem), ***Svadhisthana* Chakra** - Sex (or Water) chakra.

KLIM – (pronounce Kliim). *Kameshwari*, goddess of desire. ***Muladhara* Chakra** - Root (or Earth) chakra

Divine Grace Yoga - Mantra Shakti

Summary/reminder - Use the seed mantras as below
Aim, Hrim, Srim, Krim, Klim

AIM – (pronounce Aiim), the bija mantra of Saraswati, the goddess of learning.

HRIM (pronounced Hreem) is is the mantra of the Divine Maya. Through it we can control the illusion power of our own minds. Mahamaya is the goddess of power over the created universe (of illusion).

SHRIM (pronounced Shreem) is a mantra of love, devotion and beauty, relating to Lakshmi, the Goddess of Beauty and Divine Grace, who gives us the good things of life, including health. It aids in fertility and rejuvenation. Lakshmi is the goddess of wealth (in its broadest sense).

KRIM (pronounced Kreem) is the great mantra of Kali, has a special power relative to the lower chakras, which it can both stimulate and transform. It a main mantra of the Tantra. It should be used with care. Kali, the fierce goddess, has the power to destroy.

KLIM – (pronounce Kliim), the bija mantra of Kameshwari, the goddess of desire or contentment and satisfaction.

Practical exercises

Back to the practicalities! There's a lot of self-help books out there regarding getting well. Take the diet and supplement scene. Those books towards the end tend to put in a lot of recipes. I always avoid such books as they annoy me! (The recipes').

Here is one of my recipes! This is for relaxation which can lead to mindfulness and can also enhance meditation. When I meditate in a group, I find the presence of the group can also add to the potency of meditation and reduction of unnecessary thoughts. However, I may still get a lot of junk going on in my brain, unless I do some exercises to quieten all this noise

Relaxation is as follows. Sit or stand with both feet on the ground and visualize the body tension dissipating down through the feet into the earth. Visualize at the same time any tension being replaced by the earth's stabilizing forces filtering up through the body into the brain.
Mother Earth kindly release my tension/anxiety/disturbance.

Divine Grace Yoga - Mantra Shakti

Then for four minutes at least keep the spine straight as possible to allow energy to flow. You can see this as being scientific, in to the regarding the neurochemical/electrical activities throughout the nervous system. Or you can see it as the Kundalini energy business. Either way, the bottleneck is at the neck, and this is where tension is experienced as neck or shoulder aches or stiffness. We often block free flow of our nervous system activities, which "pools in certain areas, and then find ourselves with anxiety, or confusion. Anxiety/tension focused in the stomach or chest area, manifesting as nausea or chest tightness. Or confusion with "pooling" in the brain. The lack of free flow through the neck area can also be connected with other issues.

To get a straight spine, push chin slightly upwards if necessary, and push the shoulders back also slightly. Hold that position for up to 4 minutes or more if comfortable. If there is too much mind/body restlessness, relaxation can still take place as you pace up and down a corridor, but lifting the shoulders up, still with the visualization of allowing energies to dissipate through the feet into the earth.

Guru Yogi let me sit or be in the right posture for serenity.

Divine Grace Yoga - Mantra Shakti

Effective breathing techniques are next, which will ameliorate anxiety etc., which can drive fast and shallow breathing. All these exercise components can provide intervention also when there are some panic type symptoms. Severe panic attacks though may require more professional support, if available. There's nothing that should stop you from trying to deal with symptoms yourself, if that's your only option.

The breathing is three deep breaths in through the nose, then breathing out with an *aah* sound. You are allowing the stomach to fill on the in breath, and are pushing out the breath or squeezing in the stomach for the outgoing breath. I recommend the use of the *Soham* mantra, with the in-breathing in being *So,* and the outgoing being *Hum*. Soham is "I am That", or I am the Cosmic Consciousness or energy. *So* is the Cosmos and *Hum* is "I am". We are breathing in the universal or cosmic energy into one's whole being, then letting out the human ego based conscious worries. It's not surrendering the ego at this point. That is a different type of exercise or scenario.
I surrender to the Cosmic Energy & Consciousness.

Visualizing oneness with the cosmic energy can also be increased by pushing out with the open palms of the hand, whilst breathing out. Visualize the energy around the body as one's favorite color in a pale shade. It is an aura or a shield depending on immediate need. Or you can make it religious visualization of the Deity powers, whichever God/Goddess/ you are inclined to worship. It can be completely non-religious, or non-spiritual. You modify to suit. The colors come into your body with the in breath, surrounding you then is an aura that is also visualized as healing. (There are some options given here – its personal choice).

In Eastern religions there is a concept of having a "shield". In Sanskrit this is a *Kavach:* a shield that protects and enables one to go through life without fearfulness about what might happen. With the healing color, it can be seen as a shield, or like a sponge or an aura that soaks up and dilutes/defuses one's emotions and thoughts. It's just somewhere we can push out some of the tension or emotion that are negative troublesome and hold them somewhere suspended temporarily. This exercise can then also enable a much faster and more focused meditation practice. As soon as one sits down, the groundwork has been done, and we have actually begun the mindfulness, which then allows us to experience mindlessness in our meditation.

In our mindfulness we are stopping, stepping back, and observing. In the relaxation/focusing we are doing what we need to further place our soul energy into connection at a higher spiritual level. The next step is ideally deeper meditation. However, if that's not doable or difficult for some reason, another option is to go back into that aura or protective shell, and see what is activating any negative thoughts. Then we need to see what that is doing to us, and what change we need to make to the negative self-talk. We do this then by replacing the negative with something more balanced. Add something positive about yourself to any negative thinking that you identify

You can try to see in your aura space the obstacles to meditation. Thoughts that disturb or distract you. The plan is not to remove them, as that can take too much effort and application. Just visualize the thought train temporarily as outside and allow your shield to protect you also from others negative energies. (Longer term management of negative thinking and self-esteem may also benefit from work with a counsellor/therapist). Practice of meditation will also provide healing, as will repetition of a suitable mantra. (You might need a guru rather than a counsellor here).

In the practice of *Defusion,* you can inspect or observe your past or present or present emotions, thinking and others "interference", by putting them slightly outside ones being. In this mode you can visualize those tricky issues that distract and disturb, as being outside you in a temporary process. Put them in the clouds while you imagine you're on the mountain. Put them in the waves while you imagine you're sitting on the sand dunes, or drift past them as if you were on a boat going down a river. This Defusion is somewhat similar to dilution, (of anxiety etc. achieved during a relaxation exercise). That's all we're doing here. We're not curing anything. If you want to cure, then you will need to go further with your therapeutic processes or spiritual journey.

Here in these books, I am talking about connection with our deity or a spiritual pathway, or a particular religious belief. (Not going any deeper than into the domains of counsellors or therapists). True, we can do these exercises to help us to be now in the moment and be present mindfully. Then we can use our prayer mantra, meditation, or similar means to understand"

Who am I? What am I? What is life? What is Truth?

Divine Grace Yoga - Mantra Shakti

We then go into the whole dimension of being conscious of being part of Consciousness.

Our consciousness is part of, and the same material as, the Cosmic Consciousness.

This is why we say we are Divine.

You are Divine because we can place ourselves as inseparable from the Divine.

If God is Divine then *all* Creation must be so also!

(Where then will you then place - *evil*)?

Divine Grace Yoga - Mantra Shakti

Exercise to deal with anything, anywhere, anytime!

This exercise is a spiritual and therapeutic practice using mantras and chakra meditation to address negative thoughts, anxiety, and emotional disturbances. It involves invoking the light of the Guru to illuminate mental content, chanting specific mantras to "place" troubling content around the body in one area, and then "moving past it all.

We start with chanting: *Om Shanti* x 3
To provide a better level of calmness
Then chant *Hari Om Guru Om x 3 while* **and touching the top of the head**

The purpose is to ask for the light of the Universal Teacher (Guru) to illuminate the thoughts in the mind so that they can be seen more clearly, without judgment as being negative or positive.
Seven chakras are invoked next, visualizing going down from the Crown chakra, the third eye chakra, the throat chakra, the heart chakra, the Solar Plexus chakra, the Sacral chakra, and the Muladhara, (base of the spine), chakra.

Divine Grace Yoga - Mantra Shakti

Chant the mantras Om, (Crown & "third eye), Aiim, (throat), Hreem, (heart), Shreem, (Solar Plexus), Kreem, (Sacral), and Kleem, (base of spine).

Visualization is used for gathering thoughts and energies from the chakras. (See them releasing upwards to the Crown from each chakra).

Then touching the Crown an umbrella-like visualization is used, where all the thoughts and energies slide down the "umbrella" to be gathered around the heart area. About an arm's length away. around the body).
Chant Om Hreem as this process occurs

Dealing with negative or anxious thoughts.
Instead of fighting or blocking them, the witness and accepting the thoughts, placing them in the protective umbrella-like girdle around the heart.
Using **Om Hreem** to gain clarity.

Use the mantra 'Triim now. Push the mantra out away from the body with the right hand – palm out. (A Visualization).

Divine Grace Yoga - Mantra Shakti

Trim is a powerful mantra associated with the heart chakra and the goddess power that creates and moves through the world. It helps to push through and dissipate negative energies, emotions, and thoughts, facilitating healing and transformation.

How does the exercise relate to the concept of the inner child and parts in Internal Family Systems (IFS)?
The exercise acknowledges the presence of different parts or inner child aspects that communicate through thoughts and emotions. It encourages observing these parts without judgment and managing them by placing them around the heart area for clarity and healing.

What is the role of the heart chakra in this practice?
The heart chakra is a powerful connecting chakra that radiates cosmic energy and serves as the central area where all thoughts and energies are gathered, witnessed, and worked through.

How does the practice of this exercise help mental wellness and is it therapy?
The practice suggests that mental wellness as commonly understood is a construct and that true healing comes from accepting and working through

thoughts and emotions using mantras and meditation rather than relying solely on therapy or medication.

What advice is given for practicing this exercise regularly?
It is advised to practice the exercise anytime, especially when calm, upon waking, or before sleep, to keep the cycle going, manage stress and anxiety, and maintain clarity and healing over time.

So:

Hari Om Shanti Shanti Shanti, then Hari Om Guru Om, and I'm touching my head. Hari Om Guru Om - we want the light of the Guru so that we can see what's going on in our thoughts. Lots of thoughts, anxiety thoughts, negative self-thoughts, ruminations, all thoughts, all sorts of thoughts. So, what we're doing now is asking for the light of the Universal Teacher to lighten up that material.

We're not seeing it negative or positive. We're just going to see it clearly or there will be light shining there. So, we want to make sure we've got the whole package there in our brain because that's where they come from. But they also come from our bodies. Having got the light, the next step is to go down through the chakras to release the thoughts, the energy of the thoughts.

The negativity, the ruminations, the anxiety, plus any other thoughts that need release, which are not purposeful to us at this moment. I'm going to start with Om, and you can follow me. Om. That's the chakra here. You might like to look at where I'm putting my fingers. The Sahasrara chakra - crown chakra.

Coming down to the third eye between the eyebrows touching with the right hand with the middle finger Now we can touch with our hand going down to the heart chakra. Now we go down to the navel chakra Now we go down to the Solar Plexus and then Muladhara - at the base of the spine.

Om, aim, hrim, srim, krim, klim. That releases all the energy back up - each mantra per chakra.

So, we're back up to the Crown. Now it's all coming, we visualize all that thought pattern that you have some distress about, some concern about. It's all now coming up.
Now we visualize an umbrella, like a plastic sort of clear, but not plastic. It's a flow of data in streams.

Divine Grace Yoga - Mantra Shakti

So, we've got this "umbrella shape", all the data, and it's flowing. And now, it's all the thoughts that you want to investigate, see clearly, and maybe even deal with, possibly, or use, beneficially. So, we're going to chant Om Hrim, and we're seeing it around the heart area.

You can put your hands around your heart, chest area, Feel all that energy. It's soothing because you're witnessing it. You're not affected by it.

The content might be unpleasant, like the black data and blobs green, blobs of blue, blobs of red. It's all coming down to this space around your chest and to the back surrounding the heart. And we're just going to go Om Hrim. (Remember all the i sounds of the mantras are long – a double i).

This is similar to the exercise we did when we did the breathing and we pushed out anger and negative thoughts into the sponge, into the aura - held back by the shield that we made. Now we're doing the same thing with the chakra mantras. And we're now dealing with it from the witness perspective,

You might see certain areas/segments. You know, like on a computer, like segments on the hard drive. So, this contains anxiety. This contains trauma. This contains

Divine Grace Yoga - Mantra Shakti

ruminations of all sorts. We can apportion parts of this area around us now.

Around the heart, back, front, but about an arm's length away. And we can, if we want to, delve into those thought processes that are sitting there and say, well, what is that area for? What's that area about? If you want to, that's up to you.

Observe, see it, witness it. There might be some colors. There might be some kind of feeling/emotion about them. They all vary for each person.

But the main thing is...

You want to get to a place where you can comfortably hold whatever it is you want to deal with. But you don't have to deal with everything at once. You could be worried about something, a rumination, or you could have anxiety about something. But you can now place it here or over here or over here. It's up to you. You place it where you want it, where you can see it. You can put it behind you if you don't want to see it.

Just leave it there and wander around doing your job. It's behind me. I can't see it, so I don't know that it's there. It's up to you.

Divine Grace Yoga - Mantra Shakti

Now, this is why my main mantra is on TRIM. (As written in Sanskrit - त्रीं). Pronounced Triim or Treem. It is the Goddess Power – Shakti, that creates and goes through the world. It's actively creating.

Accepting and dealing with anything, including health. So Trim is good mantra for longevity, good health, and overcoming problems. Because you're actually not avoiding them. You're witnessing them and then you're now starting to move through them. Not blocking them. You're not necessarily dealing with them. You might be just going through them.

Suppose you've got a rumination and anxiety about something. Oh, I've seen it here. I've got it. And then you take your right hand and push into it with Trim and push through it. So, what happens then is, firstly you're coming out the other side, and then, it's being dissipated or dispersed.

That's the force that created everything. So, you're in touch with the whole creation, the female Shakti energy that created everything we see, the Maya. The Goddess who is in charge of the Maya, if you like.

So Trim is quite a powerful mantra, but you need to be ready to be engaged at that level with the world, to be able to go through it. And when you're not at that level,

Divine Grace Yoga - Mantra Shakti

it's too hard to get into that because agitation, or thought processes, or emotions are too jangly. So that's why we do the Om Shanti, Shanti, Shanti to just start. And three deep breaths.

And yes, you've got the inner child business around you, around your heart. You might put it behind you. Most people do; they bury it. But now you might want to bring it out front and you can see it. Then maybe walk through it.

And as you walk through it, it's the joy, joy of being okay with it.

You can then just be peaceful and blissful. Then, when feeling quite calm focus one the mantra sound as it tails of into a *mmmm* sound.
Go into the ether, into the cosmos,

Now in psychology we have *ego identity. But,* it is about being enmeshed in Maya, the illusion, enmeshment. It's not about identity particularly. It's more about enmeshment and holding on to thoughts, emotions, and all those things - which is fine. If we're managing them, we can hold them in our mind.

Maybe a lot of people are too bogged down in it all, so they just want mental wellness
Because they associate themselves with the mind and the mind seems sick. *But*, originally there were different concepts regarding this *mental wellness thing*. It's another recent construct. It's only in recent history that we have psychiatrists and psychologists. Never had them in the "good old days"!

I use the mantras in a very practical way, channeling them down into the chakras, which has not been done before in any of the scriptures I have read about. (There are other words associated traditionally with chakras – but for *mantra chanting*).
Nobody has said, well, take Om Guru Om, and apply it to C.B.T. techniques

And then come down to Om Hrim, like a visualization, again as in *Defusion* techniques. So, I'm applying mantras to therapy. It's a new application.
Why not? I don't want to sit on the street and switch off from the world for days. I want to be able to manage the world. Have the time to manage stress, manage the pressures of life, and manage the setbacks.
This is about using mantras in a very therapeutic way. We need practical solutions, not pills, not the therapy,

not something expensive. It's something that is within, available within us. Take responsibility for it. Take the agency for it. Know the body. I know it's able to heal. There is an ability there - if I stay out of the *fixing mode.*

Divine Grace Yoga – Mantra Shakti

This the Sanskrit Hymn I chant each morning

kumārī stōtram

jagatpūjyē jagadvandyē sarvaśaktisvarūpiṇī |
pūjāṁ gṛhāṇa kaumāri jaganmātarnamō:'stu tē 1

tripurāṁ tripurādhārāṁ trivargajñānarūpiṇīm |
trailōkyavanditāṁ dēvīṁ trimūrtiṁ pūjayāmyaham 2

kalātmikāṁ kalātītāṁ kāruṇyahṛdayāṁ śivām |
kalyāṇajananīṁ dēvīṁ kalyāṇīṁ pūjayāmyaham 3

aṇimādiguṇādharā-makārādyakṣarātmikām |
anantaśaktikāṁ lakṣmīṁ rōhiṇīṁ pūjayāmyaham 4

kāmacārīṁ śubhāṁ kāntāṁ kālacakrasvarūpiṇīm |
kāmadāṁ karuṇōdārāṁ kālikāṁ pūjayāmyaham 5

caṇḍavīrāṁ caṇḍamāyāṁ caṇḍamuṇḍaprabhañjinīm |
pūjayāmi sadā dēvīṁ caṇḍikāṁ caṇḍavikramām 6

sadānandakarīṁ śāntāṁ sarvadēvanamaskṛtām |
sarvabhūtātmikāṁ lakṣmīṁ śāmbhavīṁ pūjayāmyaham 7

durgamē dustarē kāryē bhavaduḥkhavināśinīm |
pūjayāmi sadā bhaktyā durgāṁ durgārtināśinīm 8

sundarīṁ svarṇavarṇābhāṁ sukhasaubhāgyadāyinīm |
subhadrā jananīṁ dēvīṁ subhadrāṁ pūjayāmyaham 9

iti śrī kumārī stōtram |

Divine Grace Yoga - Mantra Shakti

O worshiped by the universe, worshiped by the universe, in the form of all powers
Accept my worship, O maiden, mother of the universe, I offer my obeisance's to you 1

Tripura, the basis of Tripura, the form of knowledge forall eras
I worship the goddess Trimurti, who is worshiped in the three worlds 2

She is the soul of time, transcendental to time, and has a compassionate heart
I worship the auspicious Goddess, the mother of auspiciousness 3

Anima and other qualities are the basis of this and other *Akara* forces.
I worship the goddess Rohini, the source of infinite power 4

Lustful, auspicious, beloved, in the form of the cycle of time
I worship Kalika who bestows desires and is merciful and generous 5

I always worship Goddess Chandika who is fiercely powerful 6

She is always happy and peaceful and is worshiped by all the gods
I worship Lakshmi Shambhavi who is the embodiment of all the gods 7

In the difficult to reach (troubles), the noble, (Goddess), is the destroyer of our suffering
I always worship with devotion Durga, fortress of destruction of all our troubles. 8

Beautiful in all colors and giving happiness and fortune
I worship goddess Subhadra, the eternal Subhadra 9

कुमारी स्तोत्रम्

जगत्पूज्ये जगद्वन्द्ये सर्वशक्ति स्वरुपिणि ।
पूजा गृहाण कौमारि जगन्मातर्नमोस्तुते ॥ १ ॥

त्रीपुरां त्रिपुराधारां त्रिबर्षां ज्ञानरूपिणीम् ।
त्रैलोक्य वन्दितां देवीं त्रिमूर्ति पूजयाम्यहम् ॥ २ ॥

कालात्मिकां कलातीतां कारुण्यहृदयां शिवाम् ।
कल्याणजननीं देवीं कल्याणीं पूजयाम्यहम् ॥ ३ ॥

अणिमादिगुणाधाराम् अकाराद्यक्षरात्मिकाम् ।
अनन्तशक्तिकलां लक्ष्मीं रोहिणीं पूज्याम्यहम् ॥ ४ ॥

कामाचारीं शुभा कान्तां कालचक्रस्वरूपिणीम् ।
कामदां करुणोदारां कालिकां पूजयाम्यहम् ॥ ५ ॥

चण्डवीरां चण्डमायां चण्डमुण्डप्रभञ्जनीम् ।
पूजयामि सदा देवीं चण्डिकां चण्डविक्रमाम् ॥ ६ ॥

सदानन्दकारीं शान्तां सर्वदेव नमस्कृताम् ।
सर्वदेवात्मिकां लक्ष्मीं शाम्भवीं पूजयाम्यहम् ॥ ७ ॥

दुर्गमे दुस्तरेयार्ष्ये भवदुःखविनाशिनिम् ।
पूजयामि सदा भक्त्या दुर्गां दुर्गार्तिनाशिनीम् ॥ ८ ॥

सुन्दरीं सर्व्ववर्णाभां सुखसौभाग्यदायिनीम् ।
सुभद्राजननीं देवीं सुभद्रां पूजयाम्यहम् ॥ ९ ॥

॥ इति कुमारी स्तोत्र सम्पूर्णम् ॥

Divine Grace Yoga - Mantra Shakti

Paramhansa Swami Ganeshi Giri

1975 Gujerat India

Divine Grace Yoga - Mantra Shakti

Yogi Dream – Explanation.
(Authors acrylic art on original print)

I had this dream in 1972. I was a monk in India.

The dream was about an event circa 1925.

In the dream I was an Englishman in India, and part of the Raj ruling class.

I was out hunting tigers.

The yogi I met was sitting just outside his cave in the jungle.

He said" You will hunt no more tigers. You will love and protect tigers".

True – I do now. The tiger is my favorite animal.

Divine Grace Yoga - Mantra Shakti

The Author

In my younger years, from 1976, I was a monk in India for 10 years. (*Paramhansa Ganesh Giri*).
I was born in England in 1947 – Raymond Pattison
I have been a Mental Health Practitioner since 1980.
Get Mantra information/links to books & more on my web/blog site: www.goddessmantra.guru
Also:
Om Divine Grace - podcasts
Mantra Guru-Raymond YouTube – Kundalini tutorials.

My books are in paperback & eBooks:
English-Man, Beggar-Man, Holy-Man
My journey overland to India in 1976, & my 10 years there a monk

Divine Grace Journey
The post-India years spiritual journey plus *teachings*

Goddess Inspired - Collected Writings

Therapeutic Journeys to Self-Realisation

The Transcendental Guru

Why Spirituality?

My Mantra Art:

https://fineartamerica.com/art/raymond+pattison

Mantra for Enlightenment from:
mantraguru.raymond@gmail.com

www.ingramcontent.com/pod-product-compliance
Lightning Source LLC
Chambersburg PA
CBHW051429290426
44109CB00016B/1482